THE BUDDHIST PATH TO AWAKENING

TEJANANDA

THE BUDDHIST PATH TO AWAKENING

WINDHORSE PUBLICATIONS

Published by Windhorse Publications
11 Park Road
Birmingham
B13 8AB

Cover design Dhammarati
Cover image Buddha head, Gandhara
Printed by Interprint Ltd, Marsa, Malta

British Library Cataloguing in Publication Data:
A catalogue record for this book is available from the British Library

ISBN 1 899579 02 8

Publisher's note: Since this work is intended for a general readership, Pali and
Sanskrit words have been transliterated without the diacritical marks that would
have been appropriate in a work of a more scholarly nature.

CONTENTS

About the Author

Tejananda was born John Wakeman in London in 1949. He first became intrigued by Buddhism when, in the early 1970s, he was introduced to it during a course in world religions. Qualifying as a teacher of religious studies, he worked for several years in schools in southern England whilst pursuing his growing personal interest in Buddhism. One morning in the spring of 1975 he decided he was a Buddhist.

Learning to meditate from books, his understanding of Buddhism became clearer and his practice more directed as a result of reading Sangharakshita's *A Survey of Buddhism*. After practising Buddhism alone for some time, he encountered the Buddhist movement founded by Sangharakshita, the Friends of the Western Buddhist Order. In 1980 he was ordained as a member of the Western Buddhist Order and received the name Tejananda.

Over the past twenty years Tejananda has worked in a number of Buddhist ventures including a vegetarian restaurant and a UK charity which funds educational and social projects in India. He was also Chairman of the Bristol Buddhist Centre for six years. He has written a number of articles and booklets on aspects of Buddhism, and has been involved in the editing of Buddhist magazines.

Currently, Tejananda is a member of the resident teaching team at the Vajraloka meditation retreat centre in North Wales. He plans to start the new millennium by undertaking a three-year meditation retreat with a friend, in the highlands of Scotland.

Acknowledgements

Many thanks for stimulation and helpful criticism to Sthiramati, Hannah Manasse, Satyapala, Saccanama, and Sagaramati. My especial thanks to Elizabeth English for her constant encouragement and help, and to Brigid Avison for her generous editing work.

My gratitude also to Nagabodhi for encouraging me to write and for great patience in waiting for this book; to Padmavajri for gently keeping me on course; and to Jinananda and Shantavira for all their editing work and useful comments.

Tejananda
Vajraloka
North Wales
November 1998

INTRODUCTION

OVER THE LAST twenty to thirty years, Buddhism has become an established and growing part of virtually all Western societies. Most people nowadays would hardly lift an eyebrow in surprise to discover that a friend or colleague is a practising Buddhist. Office workers, teachers, unemployed people, plumbers, shop assistants – in fact anybody, living just about any kind of lifestyle, could well be among the thousands of Westerners now practising Buddhism.

Films, magazines, and newspapers have all reflected this developing interest, though naturally tending to focus on the more glamorous, exotic, or newsworthy aspects. But in a less dramatic way, Buddhist organizations have been opening centres and other projects in Western countries with increasing regularity over the past few decades. In the UK alone, these have more than doubled in the last ten years. Most of them offer anything from simple meditation instruction for stressed-out city dwellers to a complete Buddhist way of life.

The story of Buddhism's journey to the West began hundreds of years ago. At the end of the thirteenth century, for example, Marco Polo returned from the Far East with descriptions of Buddhist practices, and accounts continued to filter through from Christian missionaries. But despite this contact it wasn't until the early nineteenth century that Westerners were able to build up a reliable picture of Buddhist teachings, thanks to the work of a number of pioneering scholars. It was this academic exploration, rather than Buddhist missionary activity, which opened up the possibility of Westerners themselves becoming Buddhists. By the end of the nineteenth century a small number of people in Europe and America had taken that unprecedented step.

So what is it that Westerners today find attractive about Buddhism?

For one thing, many people feel encouraged and relieved to discover just how different Buddhism is from Western ideas about religion. One major difference is that it does not teach the existence of a God, let alone revolve around belief in such an entity. Another is that it does not expect people to believe things that they cannot, at least in principle, experience for themselves. At the same time, Buddhism has its own profound and inspiring spiritual vision of human potential and of the universe we live in.

REALIZING OUR POTENTIAL

Buddhism always starts from our immediate experience. It encourages us to be aware of exactly what we are and how we act. Then it points out that, whatever we are right now – even if we are angry, confused, or depressed – each and every one of us has unlimited potential. Every human being has the capacity to develop qualities such as kindness, clarity, vitality, compassion, and wisdom. If we choose to do so, we can realize, deepen, and extend these and other qualities until – ultimately – we reach the state of *Buddhahood*.

A 'Buddha' is someone who is 'awakened' or 'enlightened'. As far as Buddhists are concerned, the state of awakening is the realization not just of our highest potential as human beings but of the highest of all states of being. The metaphor of awakening or waking up is a powerful and appropriate one for the Buddhist path and its goal. Buddhist teachings often state that, compared with the awakened state, our normal human state is like being lost in a dream or in deep, unconscious sleep. Most people have probably had the experience of waking up from a vivid dream only to realize that all the things that seemed so very important a moment ago were imaginary. If we had been dreaming that we were about to be pushed over a cliff, for example, we know almost the instant we wake that there is nothing to fear. Awakening itself is said to be something like this – a quality or state combining both knowing and waking. This is a very provisional description, though. Awakening is, directly and indirectly, the subject of the whole of this book.

Until recently, Western writers tended to use 'enlightenment' more than 'awakening' to translate the Sanskrit *bodhi*. However, awakening is not only a very appropriate metaphor; it is also closer to the root meaning of *bodhi*. So that is the term we will be using in this book.

A PRACTICAL APPROACH

According to the Buddha, the way to awakening is like a raft that one constructs to get across a wide river, from danger on one side to safety on the other. What the raft is made from is not important; what really matters is whether it gets you across. Similarly, the way to awakening consists of whatever enables people to make genuine progress towards that state of awakening, whether it is 'Buddhism' or not. The Buddha also pointed out that, once you had reached the other side of the river, it would make no sense to heave the raft on to your back and carry it with you. Its purpose would have been served. Similarly, once you have realized awakening, Buddhism has served its purpose too. Buddhism is a means to an end, not an end in itself.

As a consequence, its approach to the spiritual life – the path to awakening – is entirely pragmatic. According to one traditional description, Buddhism is a 'come-and-see' teaching. It is up to each of us to test the teachings for ourselves and discover directly whether they work. In Buddhism we are not asked to accept something on someone else's say-so. If we find that a teaching or practice leads to the results it is supposed to, well and good. If it does not, even after we have given it a good try, that is not a problem – there are many other approaches we can take.

The Buddha himself asked his followers to apply their own judgement and discrimination to his teachings rather than just accept them unthinkingly. This request applies to you now, as you read this book. Do the teachings presented here seem to be obvious common sense, reasonably plausible, improbable, or just completely ridiculous? Do they accord with your experience and understanding of life? Only if a teaching passes this initial scrutiny should we test it in practice.

This does not mean, though, that everything in Buddhist teaching can be known by direct experience straight away. When people first come across the teaching on awakening, for instance, they may have a feeling or intuition that it is 'right'. Or, having considered the teaching carefully, they may decide that it seems reasonable and that such an attainment may be possible. But they cannot know this directly, in the way that we know the taste of a peach when we bite into it. However, the way to awakening is a path – a process – and the first steps on that path can be taken immediately. If the results turn out as the teaching claims, then we can reasonably assume that the next steps will do so as well – and so on, all the way up to awakening itself.

TRANSFORMING OUR WHOLE BEING

As its pragmatic nature suggests, Buddhism respects rationality – even though, as we shall see, awakening itself transcends all thoughts and concepts. Every Buddhist teaching or practice has a purpose, and that purpose can be rationally evaluated and understood within the overall scheme of the Buddhist path. At the same time, Buddhism does not reduce everything to the intellect, or claim that the world can be fully understood by the intellect alone.

Western culture is still pervaded by a strong notion – originating in the eighteenth-century intellectual movement in Europe known as the Enlightenment – that we are 'rational animals', despite a vast amount of evidence that we are far more 'animal' than 'rational'. How is it possible to look at the history of the last hundred years – or even at this evening's news – and continue to hold the view that our actions are led mainly by reason? Perhaps the strength of this belief is itself sufficient proof of our irrationality.

It is true that we are all capable of rationality, but on the whole we are not rational beings. Buddhism observes that it is our instincts and emotions that drive most of our actions – and most of our thoughts as well. This is why there is a strong emphasis on transforming these aspects of ourselves through Buddhist practices such as meditation, mindfulness, devotion, and ritual.

But though many Buddhist practices are not in themselves concerned with the rational mind, they always have a clear rationale. Ritual and other such activities can help us, if we engage in them with a clear awareness of their purpose, to explore our depths and transform ourselves there. A purely rational religion (which is how Westerners in the nineteenth century often portrayed Buddhism) would be virtually useless in terms of enabling self-transformation, as it would leave most of our being untouched. But though many Buddhist practices are non-rational in themselves, they always have a clear rationale. Only by being aware of the purpose of a specific practice can we determine whether it is a useful addition to our raft.

THE SEARCH FOR MEANING

Buddhism has often been called 'the middle way'. In a modern Western context it can be seen as a middle way between, and possibly a resolution of, two strongly opposed world-views. These are, on the one hand, the views of the monotheistic religions, particularly Christianity, and, on the other, various ideas and claims about the nature of existence that could be grouped under the term 'scientific materialism'. Both these perspectives are now unacceptable to an increasing number of Westerners.

A significant number of people, even if they find some aspects of Christian teaching attractive or meaningful, encounter elements that present an obstacle to their becoming (or remaining) Christians. Some, for example, cannot accept the New Testament account of Christ's death and resurrection as both historical fact and the sole source of religious salvation for all humanity – especially since it leads many Christians to believe that Christianity is the only true religion.

Whatever their reasons, many Westerners today have rejected the moral and spiritual authority of traditional Western religions. This rejection has been expressed in two particularly extreme forms: atheism and materialism. Militant atheism, focusing on arguments against the existence of God, seems to be unfashionable these days; but materialism, and particularly what we could broadly refer to as scientific materialism, has become an orthodoxy in the modern West, its ideas pervading society in many ways.

Scientific materialism is not to be confused with science as such. Science proper is a methodology, dealing with objective, measurable data. Its concern is to develop and test theories that provide an understanding of this empirical data. Scientific materialism, on the other hand, is a philosophy based on the belief that nothing exists except that which can be explained by scientific methodology. Its more recent form, physicalism, holds that physics will one day be able to account for all phenomena whatsoever. Thus, if there is anything that cannot be understood in scientific terms – and spiritual experience is an obvious example – then scientific materialism is obliged to deny its validity or, what amounts to the same thing, to explain it as a product of brain activity.

Surprisingly, scientific materialism has more in common with Christianity than with science. Though often espoused by scientists, it is not itself scientific. It is a belief. Science has enormous power and kudos in our society, and scientific materialism basks in this, presenting itself as science when it is in fact much more like theology – a rationale for beliefs that are held to be given, objective facts. Nevertheless, scientific materialism influences the world-view of countless people. Part of this world-view is that life is essentially pointless, meaningless, and valueless; but such a view has itself been rejected by many people, who find it inconsistent with the deeper, spiritual levels of their own and others' experience.

Contrasted with monotheistic religion and scientific materialism, Buddhism presents an outlook on life and reality that is both reasonable and emotionally satisfying. Crucially, it presents ways in which, from the very beginning, every individual can positively check the truth – or otherwise – of its views of ourselves and the world we live in.

AN ETHICAL FRAMEWORK

Buddhism also provides a realistic approach to the ethical problems of our time. The moral regeneration of Western society is a vital and urgent issue. For many, the loss of religion is tantamount to the loss of a basis for ethical behaviour. Without God, without Christianity, some ask, where is moral authority to come from? If there is no Divine Lawgiver, is morality relative rather than absolute, and explained, for example, as a function of biological evolution? In societies steeped in the values of Buddhism, such a question would not even arise. Buddhism teaches a sophisticated and effective ethical basis for human action and interaction that does not rely for its authority on a transcendental judge (see page 47).

More than this, in its teaching of non-dogmatic tolerance of others' lifestyles and points of view – spiritual and otherwise – Buddhism provides a viable basis for inter-personal, inter-racial, and international harmony. It fosters lifestyles that are moderate, low-consumption, and ecologically sustainable. Its extraordinarily rich range of traditions and approaches has already proved itself adaptable to the conditions of life – and the needs of people – in the West today. All this will be explored and explained in the course of this book.

In the following chapters I have attempted to paint a broad-brush picture of Buddhism that I hope will be recognized as a true likeness by the majority of Buddhists, even if it necessarily leaves out a lot of the fascinating detail. Nevertheless, the book naturally represents my own view and understanding of Buddhism. At the same time, apart from what I have experienced directly, I owe my perceptions, perspectives, and understandings of Buddhism to others – to the writers of the many books on Buddhism I have read; to other Buddhists; to members of my own Buddhist community, the Western Buddhist Order; and above all to my teacher, Sangharakshita. The book reflects these influences.

1

THE BUDDHA

EVERY HUMAN BEING is a potential Buddha.

It is worth restating this, as it is one of the most significant of all Buddhist teachings. The highest goal of Buddhism – awakening or enlightenment – can be gained by anybody. It is not limited to just a few, special, saintly people. All human beings can become Buddhas as long as they can muster the determination, wholeheartedness, and commitment that the task requires. Awakening is achievable, and each of us can make significant progress towards it in a comparatively short period of time.

But what is awakening? The Buddhist tradition has always recognized that awakening is essentially indescribable, whether in words, concepts, or images. This might suggest that any attempt to understand awakening is a fruitless task, but fortunately this is not the case. Words, images, concepts, symbols, imagination, feeling, and empathy are just some of the means or faculties at our disposal. Properly cultivated and directed, these faculties can take us a long way towards understanding awakening and realizing it for ourselves. Buddhism starts, very practically, with the materials that lie to hand.

The teachings of Buddhism – and the words, images, and symbols through which they are communicated – are sometimes likened to a 'finger pointing at the moon'. If somebody tries to point out the moon to you, you won't see it if you fix your gaze on the finger. It is important not to let the means to awakening become ends in themselves. For example, someone could develop such an enthusiasm for studying the history and teachings of the many different schools of

Buddhism that they forget its real purpose, which is to enable them to become awakened.

But from a slightly different perspective, the image has a further meaning: without the finger, we might never look up and see the moon in the first place. The Buddhist teachings about awakening must not mistaken for awakening itself; yet without them we would be left in the dark.

So Buddhism acts as a medium through which awakening can be approached, and it does this in two ways. Firstly, Buddhism enables us to understand awakening, at least as far as awakening can be understood by the unawakened mind; secondly, it enables us to move towards that awakening. The essence of the Buddhist approach to awakening in both these senses is embodied in what are traditionally called the Three Jewels.

The Three Jewels (so called to suggest their great rarity and value) represent three spiritual principles. The first is the Buddha – the awakened one – embodying the principle of awakening; the second is the Dharma, which is both the truth that awakening embodies and the way to awakening; and the third is the Arya-Sangha, the community of the Buddha's awakened followers.

In reality, the Three Jewels are, so to speak, facets of a single jewel, the jewel of awakening. But in our unawakened state we distinguish three separate jewels: the Buddha Jewel shining with an all-encompassing golden light; the Dharma Jewel shining with brilliant, penetrating blue light; and the Sangha Jewel shining with a deep, warm red light. Between them, they embody all the teachings and practices essential to Buddhism – that is, essential to the understanding and realization of awakening.

THE BUDDHA'S PATH TO AWAKENING

'Buddha', as explained in the Introduction, is not a personal name, but a title or epithet, meaning 'one who is awakened', or 'the Enlightened One'. As a generic term, it applies to any awakened being, but references to 'the Buddha' signify the historical founder of Buddhism. The Buddha's own name was Siddhartha Gautama, and 'Buddha' is just one of several titles by which he was known after his awakening. Other titles include Jina or 'Conqueror', Arhant or 'Worthy One', and Tathagata, loosely translated as 'Thus-Gone One' – that is, the one who has gone from the unawakened state to the awakened state.

Siddhartha Gautama was born about 2,400 years ago. His family belonged to the ruling caste of the Shakya clan, which lived in an area now partly in northern India and partly in southern Nepal. His family name was Gautama, and his personal name Siddhartha. Raised by a well-off and fond – perhaps over-fond – family, he was by his own account spoiled: 'I was delicate, most delicate.... Lotus ponds were made for me at my father's house solely for my benefit.... I used no sandalwood that was not from Benares.... My garments were all of Benares cloth.' He was raised to be a future ruler of his clan and educated in military arts and the ways of leadership. At an early age he was married to a young woman called Yashodhara, and several years later they had a son.

Despite his comfortable lifestyle, the young Siddhartha found himself increasingly plagued by feelings of discontent. His response to these feelings could easily have been to seek distraction through pleasure or politics – options that were open to him and which his family positively encouraged him to pursue. But Siddhartha was a robust character with a tenacious and enquiring mind. Rather than losing himself in distraction, he was led by his inner discomfort towards a fundamental questioning of the purpose and meaning of his life.

This was exactly what his father had feared, ever since an astrologer's prediction that Siddhartha would grow up to be either a great king or a great holy man. He had taken care to insulate Siddhartha from suffering, keeping him within the protected circle of privilege, pleasure, and power. But Siddhartha, though young and healthy, became more and more deeply occupied with existential questions, particularly the implications of disease, old age, and death.

His existential crisis is vividly portrayed in the well-known legend of 'the four sights'. The story goes that Siddhartha persuades the family charioteer to take him for trips into the local town of Kapilavastu in defiance of his father's command to remain within the palace. On his first three visits, he sees sights that shake him to the core: someone old and wizened, someone desperately sick, and a corpse. Many years later, the Buddha described his youthful realization of the implications of his own mortality: 'I thought, "When an untaught ordinary man, who is subject to death, sees another who is dead, he is shocked and disgusted, forgetting that he himself is no exception. But I too am subject to death." Considering this, the intoxication of life entirely left me.'

Such reflections inevitably led Siddhartha's mind in the very direction that his family had not wanted it to go. He realized that he did not have to accept the life that had been planned for him and, according to the legend, one more chariot ride brought him face to face with his future. This was the sight of a religious wanderer who had abandoned his worldly possessions in order to devote himself to the quest for spiritual truth. India was then, as now, full of such wandering truth-seekers: meditators, ascetics, yogis, devotees of various gurus, all seeking truth or awakening in their diverse ways. It became clear to Siddhartha that this was the only direction that offered even the possibility of answers to his questions. Though he knew it would not be easy to go against the wishes of his family and to leave both them and his privileged lifestyle behind, he made up his mind: he would 'go forth from the household life to the homeless life', renounce all his worldly ties, titles, and possessions, and become a wandering truth-seeker.

So, at the age of twenty-nine, Siddhartha exchanged his fine garments for the rags of a wanderer and embarked on his quest. He sought out a renowned meditation teacher, whose approach he studied and practised with enthusiasm and energy. Within a very short time he attained a deeply blissful meditative state – a state which seemed to take him completely beyond the world and its concerns. But disappointment soon set in. In meditation, ignoring his outer senses, he could enter a blissful mystical state of inner union. But afterwards, the questions raised by old age, disease, and death were still waiting for him, unanswered. So Siddhartha decided to go forth again, leaving his first guru and approaching another. But the results were very similar, and Siddhartha had to conclude that deep meditation, powerful though it was, was not the answer. He decided to try a different approach altogether and joined a group of ascetics, practising austerities.

After several years with this group, during which he pushed himself further and punished himself more extremely than any of the others, Siddhartha started practising an austerity that consisted, in effect, of systematic starvation. One day he collapsed from weakness, and as he lay on the ground unable to get up, he realized that, far from being any nearer to awakening and the meaning of life, he was rapidly approaching a self-inflicted death. In that moment he had to conclude that austerities, too, were not going to lead him to the truth.

Siddhartha had little choice but to acknowledge that, so far, his quest had failed completely: he was no wiser than when he started. This crisis was the turning point of Siddhartha's quest. A less determined person might have been tempted to give up altogether. Siddhartha could easily have made a living as a guru – he already had an admiring group of five ascetics who were impressed by his extreme austerities. He could even have gone back to the unsatisfying but available comfort of his family. But, characteristically, he did neither of these things. Instead, he accepted that his approaches had led him only to failure. India might be full of truth-seekers but no one, it appeared, knew what the truth was. He saw that if he was to realize it – whatever it was – he would have to continue alone. Spurred by these reflections, he renounced the practices of the past five or six years, took food to restore his strength, and walked off into the jungle, alone.

Siddhartha did not try to force any new approach; he simply walked from place to place asking villagers for food and meditating under shady trees. But as he did so, something began to stir within the depths of his mind. Eventually, a childhood memory surfaced: he remembered a hot afternoon, sitting quietly in the shade of a tree, watching his father ploughing a nearby field. He had spontaneously and naturally entered a meditative state of consciousness in which he was deeply, blissfully concentrated but also lucidly aware of his surroundings and of the flux of his own mental and emotional processes. Siddhartha immediately felt that this was the key. Without hesitation, he decided to put it to the test. Finding a quiet and beautiful spot, he sat down in the cool of the evening to meditate under a great fig tree.

Anyone passing that spot in the dusk would have seen, if they noticed anything at all, only a gaunt, rag-clad figure, sitting motionless in meditation. If they had happened to pass the same way the following morning, exactly the same scene would have met their eyes. But although nothing had apparently changed during those hours, everything had changed. The most momentous single event in human history had occurred. Siddhartha Gautama had sat down there, the evening before, an ordinary human being; but now he sat there a fully awakened being: a Buddha.

What had happened? When he sat down to meditate, Siddhartha already had a disciplined and supple mind, the positive result of the past six years of spiritual training. It was not difficult for him to recreate the meditative state that he recalled from his childhood. This was very different from the states he had experienced under the instruction of his two teachers. Those had been superconscious mystical absorptions, states of ecstatic inner unification that involved complete withdrawal, not just from the senses but also from the thinking faculty of the mind. The meditative state he now entered did not involve this kind of withdrawal. It was just as he remembered: lucid, pleasurable, and highly concentrated. At the same time, his mind and senses were open to both inner and outer experience, but as different from their 'normal' state as a powerful laser is from a flickering candle.

Channelling the mental and emotional energies of his entire being, Siddhartha discovered a faculty that seemed more powerful than the sum of its parts – even, somehow, more powerful than the sum of *his* parts. As the hours passed, he focused this faculty on himself, on the world, on birth, death, rebirth, pleasure, pain, sorrow, and joy. As he did so, he found that he could penetrate and fully comprehend whatever he brought to mind. He could see into the very essence of things, and found that he was also seeing *through* them.

This seeing into and through things (or 'insight') was much more than rational understanding. It was not a matter of simply thinking things through. Siddhartha had already spent years pondering on the problems of life in the ordinary way and it had got him nowhere. What happened that night – the experience of awakening – was in a sense so obvious, and yet so unlike our usual experience, that it is very difficult to grasp or to describe. In fact, words are quite inadequate to the task.

THE PROBLEM WITH LANGUAGE

Millions upon millions of words have been spoken or written about awakening. But we have seen that, according to Buddhist tradition, the essence of awakening cannot be described by words, concepts, or images. This calls for some explanation, especially as religions are notorious for asking us to accept things 'on trust'.

Looking at our everyday experiences, though, how many of them can we capture in words? For example, we happily say things like

'That's a nice red apple' and other people know what we mean. But if we were to try to use words or concepts to convey our experience of the scent or taste of an apple, or of the colour red, or even if we tried to convey our experience of 'niceness', we would soon run up against the limitations of those words, concepts, and images. Language is simply unable to convey much of our ordinary, everyday experience. In practice, we just accept this as a fact of life. Language is abstract and symbolic and we know not to confuse it with experience itself.

With awakening, the same limitations apply, with added complications. We may get some idea of the problem if we imagine trying to convey our experience of life to someone from a two-dimensional universe in which only the sense faculties of touch and hearing exist. However brilliant our use of metaphors and analogies, they would pick up only the vaguest ideas about life in our universe.

In our attempts to understand awakening, we are in much the same position as the unfortunate two-dimensional being. The awakened state is like a higher dimension of mind, being, or awareness, and language can at best give us only a shadowy approximation of its nature. But despite these inherent limitations, words do offer us a chance to get at least an impression of awakening, using similes, parallels, images, concepts, and all the other resources available to us.

THE EXPERIENCE OF INSIGHT

The arising of insight – seeing into and seeing through things – was the crucial and, according to Buddhist tradition, the unprecedented leap in human experience which Siddhartha Gautama proved possible. It was this that made the Buddha's realization and teaching so completely different from the other spiritual paths taught at that time (and, for that matter, since).

The meaning of insight in Buddhism can be approached through an analogy: the experience of 'seeing through' a person or thing. For example, if we are watching a conjurer, we know that we are witnessing mere illusions even though they appear 'real'. In part, of course, we want to be convinced that something magical is happening. But if we find out how a particular trick works, we can no longer be taken in by it; if we see the same conjuring trick again, we see through it immediately.

Seeing through a person or thing is, of course, rather more traumatic than seeing through a conjuring trick. We might realize that someone we trusted has been manipulating us, or we might see through our justification for behaving in a particular way. Disillusion of this kind is often painful but, as the word disillusion suggests, it does at the same time involve freedom or liberation from what was really an illusion.

At their own level, insights of the disillusioning kind can lead to major and positive changes in people's lives. We often eventually acknowledge that we are wiser for such experiences. Siddhartha's insight, however, was of an entirely different order. What he saw through was not a person, a thing, or a delusion. He saw through *everything*: not only the problems that had been tormenting him, but the whole of existence.

As the night of his awakening deepened, Siddhartha began to see with unerring clarity that throughout his life (in fact through a beginningless succession of lives) he had fundamentally misunderstood, or misperceived, both himself and the world around him. He realized it was this 'wrong seeing' of things which had made life so oppressive and unsatisfying.

Along with this ever-deepening insight came a sense of growing relief and delight, then joy, and finally unshakeable bliss – the bliss that comes with complete liberation from delusion. He knew that the causes of his sense of oppression had lost their power over him. From his new perspective, his questions about life and death were questions no longer. As dawn began to light the surrounding countryside, it seemed to Siddhartha that he had at last woken from a long, troubled dream. He was now a Buddha.

For some weeks he remained in the vicinity of the tree under which the great awakening had taken place (a descendant of this 'bodhi tree' – the tree of awakening – still shades the spot). It seems that he needed time to continue absorbing the momentous change that had taken place in him. He also needed time to search for words which, however inadequately, might express his insight to others. The need to do so was growing in him continually: so powerful was the relief, bliss, and joy of his awakening, and so acute his sense of the needless, self-inflicted suffering of unawakened people, that the urge to help others to awaken was irresistible.

THE BUDDHA'S FIRST STUDENTS

But how did the Buddha communicate his awakening to others? According to tradition, the first people he approached were the five ascetics who had so admired the extremes of his asceticism. The recently awakened Buddha sought them out because, of all the people he knew, they had the strongest potential to realize awakening. When the ascetics saw the Buddha coming towards them, the story goes, they decided to be polite but not too friendly; after all, as far as they were concerned, he was a backslider – a man who had given up the spiritual quest and returned to the worldly life. However, their resolve soon crumbled: they could not help responding warmly and respectfully towards this strangely and impressively changed Siddhartha. Even so, it took the Buddha some time to convince them that he had achieved the goal that they believed could be reached only by practising austerities.

As soon as he had gained their confidence, the Buddha tried to convey the nature of his insight and awakening to them – not just theoretically, but in such a way as to enable them to realize it for themselves. The impression given by the best-known text on this event is that the Buddha sat down and delivered a sort of talk or sermon. Other texts suggest, more realistically, that the Buddha may have spent weeks meditating and intensely communicating with the ascetics. Probably he had to do a great deal of reflecting and thinking out loud in order to find words that were at all adequate to the task, given the essentially ineffable nature of his insight. However, his intuition about the ascetics proved correct. Ultimately, insight arose in one of them – Kondanna – and seeing this the Buddha jubilantly cried 'Kondanna knows! Kondanna knows!'

This moment of Kondanna's insight is one of the most celebrated and important in the Buddha's life story. It confirmed that the Buddha's insight was indeed communicable, and that others, too, could become awakened. This is exactly what happened, within a relatively short time, to the other ascetics. Each in turn, like Kondanna, developed insight; and before they and the Buddha went their separate ways, all five had realized full awakening, just as the Buddha had. There was only one difference, though it is a difference which distinguishes the Buddha not just from the five ascetics but from all other Buddhists in history: the Buddha had realized awakening alone, whereas the five ascetics were able to do so only with the help of the Buddha's teaching.

We don't know the exact nature and content of the Buddha's communication with the ascetics over the weeks or months they were together. However, there is a relatively early text describing these events that may summarize some of the Buddha's earliest teaching in a formalized way. In this account, the Buddha begins by teaching the five ascetics 'the four truths' (often called 'the four noble truths', though the original expression means something more like 'the four truths of the noble ones'). This teaching is one of the principal expressions of the Buddha's insight, and it remains central to the teachings of virtually all Buddhist traditions.

THE RELATIONSHIP BETWEEN THE FOUR TRUTHS

THE FOUR TRUTHS		
1	**Suffering**	The potential for dissatisfaction and pain is always present. This includes physical pain, mental and emotional distress, loss, not getting what we want, and fear of death. Also, a general sense of unsatisfactoriness, unfulfilment, or meaninglessness
2	**The origin of suffering**	We create suffering for ourselves through craving (and aversion) arising from our deluded self-view – relating to life mainly in terms of our own needs and wants
3	**The end of suffering**	The possibility of awakening from our deluded state – seeing through our delusion completely and permanently
4	**The way to awakening**	There is a path that leads from the unawakened to the awakened state, the noble eightfold path

Before looking at the four truths individually, it is important to understand their structure – how they relate to each other and why they take the form they do. From our own unawakened viewpoint, insight sees into two things: into the unawakened state and into the awakened state. The process that each of us has to go through, in moving from the unawakened to the awakened state, involves developing both these aspects of insight. There are four stages to the process. To begin with, we need to develop an understanding of what it means to be unawakened; this will allow us to see through our unawakened state. We also need to develop our understanding of what it means to be awakened, and then to move towards the awakened state.

Before we begin this process, it is as though we are in a deep hypnotic trance, but do not realize it. We go about our daily affairs in this trance-like state, and to us it seems like reality. To snap out of it, we need first to realize that we are in a trance and to see it for what it is. The second step is to identify what has put us into this trance. The third step is to realize that we can choose to wake up; after all, if something is keeping us in a trance, then it must be possible to wake up from it by applying an antidote. And so, in the fourth step, we apply this antidote in order to wake from our trance.

Interestingly, the underlying structure of the four truths derives from the traditional medical procedure in the Buddha's time: firstly, identify the disease; secondly, establish its cause; thirdly, affirm the possibility of health; and fourthly, prescribe a regimen that counteracts the cause and leads back to health.

THE FIRST TRUTH: SUFFERING

The first truth expresses the Buddha's insight into the nature of the unawakened state: that it is characterized by suffering. This suffering takes various forms: the physical pain of disease or injury, mental and emotional distress, the pain of loss or not getting what we want, and the fear of death. In a more general sense, there is the depressing sense of unsatisfactoriness, unfulfilment, or meaninglessness that can afflict even young, well-off, and healthy people – as Siddhartha himself had found. The unawakened cannot avoid suffering – the Buddha taught – because they live in a way that brings suffering upon themselves.

This truth of suffering may seem arguable at first. After all, most people find life very good sometimes, and many, particularly those of us living in Western societies, have little experience of the extremes of suffering that have afflicted the rest of humanity. Indeed, Western societies (like Siddhartha's family) put a great deal of effort into keeping real suffering, as well as death, away from general view (this in itself is worth reflecting upon). But in teaching the truth of suffering, the Buddha was not claiming that everybody always experiences life as unsatisfactory, let alone as continuously painful. Instead, he was pointing to the fact that the potential for dissatisfaction and pain is always there; moreover, because we are ignorant of the basic causes of suffering, we are constantly acting in ways that make it unavoidable.

THE SECOND TRUTH: THE ORIGIN OF SUFFERING

No living being wishes to suffer. One way or another, we spend most of our time trying to avoid suffering and find happiness. The problem is that we are going about it in completely the wrong way. The second truth shows us how we create suffering for ourselves by seeking its opposite.

This takes us to the essence of the Buddhist critique of the unawakened human state. On the night of his awakening, the Buddha saw that all human beings bring suffering upon themselves because of their craving. In essence, craving is a continual longing for things to be other than they are. When we are hot, we long to be cool; when we are cold, we long for warmth. When we are working, we long to be on holiday; when we are on holiday, we may wish we had gone somewhere else, or wish the holiday would never end. In both large and small ways, we give rise to such dissatisfaction and longing all the time. This craving and longing arises because, at root, we relate to other people and to the world in a biased and unrealistic way.

This bias is usually described as 'self-view'. It is the belief that we exist as a 'self' in the sense of a permanent, unchanging entity. We will explore this more fully in Chapter 7; for now, we can sum it up as ego-orientation. We each experience life as it relates to *us*: to our needs and wants. Each of us is at the centre of our own universe. Naturally, we want to be happy and to avoid suffering. This is quite healthy in itself, but then our underlying ego-orientation distorts the picture, and – consciously or unconsciously – we make assumptions such as 'I have a right to continual happiness and freedom from suffering', 'Things should always go the way I want them to', 'Other people should not get in my way'.

By pointing this out, the Buddha was not saying that people continually behave like monsters of egotism. Human beings are capable of selfless as well as selfish behaviour – if it were otherwise, awakening would not even be a possibility. The Buddha's point was that, for most of us, the self-centred view predominates. We can see this most clearly if, rather than looking for extremes of behaviour, we contemplate the minor irritations and frustrations that bedevil our daily lives.

For example, we are late and in a hurry to get somewhere. It's pouring with rain and we cannot get across the street to our car because there is so much traffic; once we are in our car, other drivers seem happy to crawl along at 15 miles an hour and unreasonably hoot at us when we cut in front of them; arriving at the station, we find that the train is running half an hour late and, when it does arrive, there's nowhere to sit.... By the time we reach our destination, we are thoroughly jangled and in a foul mood.

Such little frustrations can be multiplied endlessly in our daily experience and are exacerbated by emotions such as anxiety, pride, envy, and fear. At times they can also become much stronger and more serious. The feelings associated with small frustrations and the feelings that result in violence, murder, and war differ in degree rather than in kind.

Most of us, most of the time, are quite unaware of the selfish or egotistic assumptions that underlie our behaviour. When we have worked ourselves up into a state, it seems as though everybody and everything is gleefully conspiring to make things as difficult and unpleasant for us as possible. But the Buddha's crucial insight was that it is not the rest of the universe which is askew, but ourselves: that most human suffering is caused by the disparity between our deeply-rooted assumptions and expectations, and the way things really are. This is the very core of our unawakened state. Because of this delusion, there are two main ways in which we respond to situations in order to make them conform with our desire to be happy and avoid suffering. Actively, we respond with either craving or aversion. Passively, we respond with delusion itself, in the form of ignorance or indifference.

So if we perceive something as pleasant and enjoyable, we will tend to desire it, or, if it appears very attractive, crave it. We will then try to grasp it and possess it, making it in effect part of ourselves, part of our ego-identity. If, on the other hand, we find something unpleasant or threatening, we will feel revulsion or, in extreme cases, hatred. We will try to reject or repulse it, not wanting it to be part of us or anything to do with us. Effectively, both these tendencies can be reduced to craving: to have what we want, and not to have what we do not want. But if we encounter something that does not seem to affect us, in the sense that we neither crave it nor feel aversion towards it, then our response is indifference and we ignore it.

Craving, aversion, and delusion are inseparable from each other. Craving and aversion not only arise from delusion, but also continually feed back into it and reinforce it. In this way we keep our delusion in good repair and carry on forming and re-forming our delusion-based self-view or ego-identity.

It is not difficult to see how craving, aversion, and delusion (including delusion manifesting as indifference) are out of accord with the way things really are, and how through them we bring suffering upon ourselves. In the case of craving, for example, however much we long for something, there is nothing in the nature of the universe that guarantees we will get it. That is the way things are. In the case of aversion, however much energy we put into hating the very idea of getting old or ill, or into denying the possibility of death or of losing people and things that are dear to us, such denial is useless. Loss and death are part of life. As for things that do not impinge on our ego-identity, they can also give rise to suffering because, however indifferent we are to them, they may not be indifferent to us. The dog we ignored as we passed it could even now be running up to bite our leg!

Looking at these instances, it may seem obvious that we often go about things in a way that sets up trouble for ourselves. We may well think that, yes, probably it would be better if we lived differently. But seeing this in theory and carrying it out in practice are very different things. However well we understand the idea that deluded craving and aversion lead to suffering, any attempt to *force* ourselves into not craving or hating, simply on the basis of this theoretical understanding, would be doomed to failure. Indeed, all of us have probably done this innumerable times: 'Smoking is pathetic, I'm definitely giving up,' 'So what that my lover has left me, I'm just going to cheer up.' Usually such stratagems do not work. Even courses of therapy, carefully worked-out life plans, or irrevocable vows might be as likely to fail as to succeed.

This is because our approach to our problems is invariably far too superficial. Our fundamental delusion is not susceptible to half-hearted wishes that we could somehow be better people. What was unique about the Buddha's insight was that he saw beyond the symptoms of the human malaise and got down to the root of the problem. He saw that we will just go on doing the same old things in the same old way unless we get rid of our delusion completely.

This brings us to the third and fourth truths, embodying the Buddha's insight into the awakened state.

THE THIRD TRUTH: THE END OF SUFFERING

If the first two truths were all that Buddhism had to say about the world, it would present a very bleak picture. However, they represent only the first aspect of the Buddha's insight, his insight into the unawakened state. The first two truths are crucially important to the Buddha's teaching. They are not just saying 'things are pretty awful': they show exactly *why* things are as they are. And understanding that something is wrong, and why it is wrong, is the key to discovering how to put it right.

The third truth, often translated as 'the cessation of suffering', presents us with the possibility of awakening from our deluded state and gives us a vision of what it means to be awakened. As we have seen, we create suffering for ourselves because of our delusion. If delusion were no longer at the core of our being, our habitually egocentric way of relating to the world would cease, and the suffering it causes would cease as well.

A fully awakened person is one who has seen through their funda-mental delusion completely and permanently. They no longer expe-rience a sense of a really existing, permanent self as the centre of their being (let alone as the centre of the universe). This self-view has been seen through as a totally unnecessary, as well as highly unsatisfactory, way of relating to the world. Seeing through self-view means that it is simply no longer there, and no longer able to influence or inform the way we behave. Without the fertile soil of delusion, the 'ego-forming' reactions to life – craving and aversion – are completely uprooted. And with this fundamental change in motivation comes an end to the suffering caused by craving and aversion.

This state is called *nirvana*, a Sanskrit word that suggests the 'going out' of a fire when all its fuel has been exhausted. It suggests the freedom from inner conflict and ineffable peace that arises when delusion has been fully comprehended. Sometimes, Western writers on Buddhism have mistakenly understood nirvana to mean that no aspect or element of an awakened person remains after death – just a sort of black hole. It has also been wrongly understood as a kind of Buddhist equivalent of Heaven – a place where good Buddhists go after they die. Both these interpretations miss the mark. Nirvana is simply a metaphor that enables unawakened people to get a feel for this particular aspect of the awakened state: that there is no more fuel of self-view to maintain the fires of craving, aversion, and delusion.

What is an Awakened Person Like?

The metaphor of nirvana is a helpful pointer to the nature of awakening, but there are many other perspectives, as we will try to demonstrate. A particularly important one, not least because we can relate it to our unawakened experience, concerns the main qualities that characterize an awakened person. These are the qualities of wisdom and compassion. Wisdom and compassion can be seen as being for the awakened person what delusion, craving, and aversion are for the unawakened – the root or core of their being. These two qualities are, of course, diametrically opposed to craving, aversion, and delusion.

This wisdom is not the worldly wisdom that comes from ordinary knowledge and experience; neither is it a state of omniscience that knows every fact in the universe, however trivial. It is the result of insight. Indeed, insight and wisdom do not really differ in nature. Insight is the process of seeing through things, while wisdom is the state of having seen through them. Wisdom in the fullest sense knows things as they really are, in their own nature, without the slightest hint of delusion. To convey – or even suggest – the nature of wisdom in terms that can be understood by the unawakened mind is, as we have seen, a problematic task. Nevertheless, the Buddhist tradition has never been reticent in attempting the impossible, as will become apparent when we examine the teachings on wisdom (Chapter 7).

In the awakened state, wisdom and compassion are not separate qualities – they are even more closely related than the two sides of a coin. The Buddha's compassion found expression in his unstinting care and concern for the welfare of others. This motivation characterized his whole life after his awakening, fuelling his determination to communicate his liberating realization to others.

At first the Buddha doubted whether this was even possible: he had not yet found words that could indicate the nature of awakening; and even if he did, he was not sure whether there was anyone who would understand him. But as we saw earlier, his determination to try was rewarded with success as, one by one, the five ascetics attained the state of awakening themselves. For the rest of his life the Buddha tirelessly carried on doing the same thing: showing others the way to awakening. He continually refined and developed his teaching, and ensured that it would be passed on for the benefit of future generations.

Such selfless activity will be found in the life of anybody who has attained awakening. But the reason for the intimate link between wisdom and compassion may not at first be obvious. After all, why should awakened people not keep awakening to themselves, disappear into a mountain cave, and spend the rest of their lives enjoying the bliss of nirvana?

The reason lies in what happens when a person sees through their delusion and ceases to act out of craving and aversion. The self-centred way of relating to the world is no longer present, and with it disappear craving, aversion, and delusion; in their place, selfless qualities blossom. Where there was once a compulsive urge towards craving and grasping, now there is selfless generosity. Where there was once revulsion and hatred, now there is only unqualified love and kindness towards other beings. And where once there was delusion, now there is wisdom.

Of course, qualities such as kindness, generosity, and love are not exclusive to those who are fully awakened. But for unawakened people, self-transcendence is temporary, and these positive qualities are compromised by delusion and its associated self-oriented reactions. An awakened person, by contrast, can act only from selfless qualities so that, when they encounter suffering, their response is inevitably one of selfless compassion.

Another way of understanding the relation between wisdom and compassion takes us deep into the mysteries of the awakened state. Wisdom arises from seeing not just through our delusion of self-view, but through all such delusions. In effect, we would realize that there is no such really existent thing as a 'self' anywhere. A result of this realization is that we would no longer regard ourselves as separate, exclusive *subjects*, and other people and things as equally separate, exclusive *objects*. Instead, we would see things in a completely new way, which can be described as 'non-dual'. This does not mean that an awakened person sees subject and objects as identical; rather, non-duality in the Buddhist sense means that all beings and things in the universe are seen to be integrally connected or 'interpenetrating'. We would no longer identify with 'myself' as separate from everybody and everything else.

It is very difficult even to imagine what it might be like to experience life in this way, so different is it from our unawakened experience. But returning to the compassion element of awakening, non-duality means that, with no sense of separateness between self and others, an awakened person cannot but experience a profound empathy and sympathy with the joys and sorrows of unawakened people; and the response to those sorrows is a spontaneous and immediate upwelling of compassion.

Whilst wisdom and compassion are the principal qualities of the awakened mind, they are by no means the only ones. There are innumerable others. We have already mentioned love, kindness, and generosity. Other qualities include patience, forbearance, limitless energy, and perfect equanimity. These are important both in their own right and as aspects of compassion. They are indispensable to compassionate action, and enable the awakened person to respond appropriately to any situation.

THE FOURTH TRUTH: THE WAY TO AWAKENING

The insight encapsulated in the Buddha's fourth truth is that there is a way or path that leads from the unawakened to the awakened state. This truth also offers an outline of the path, because the Buddha did not just intuit that a path existed – he realized that path for himself and saw that it could be communicated to others. Indeed, he saw that any human being could follow it in order to become a Buddha, just as he had.

The path invariably outlined in the context of the fourth truth is that known as the 'noble eightfold path'. However, the essential principle of the fourth truth is simply 'the path' – the fact that a path exists. Which particular version of the path we follow is of secondary importance. The following chapter looks at several, including the eightfold path.

THE BUDDHA AFTER HIS AWAKENING

The remainder of the Buddha's life – some forty-five years – was a continual unfoldment of the implications of his awakening. Except during the rainy season, when travel was difficult, he spent most of his time walking the dusty tracks of northern India. Wherever he went, he attempted to communicate the path to awakening to the people he encountered. He would engage with anyone – rulers, outcasts, religious mendicants, lepers – as long as they were willing to engage with him. Not everybody was. One wanderer, recorded as the first person to encounter the Buddha after his awakening, was so struck by the Buddha's serene and radiant appearance that he couldn't help asking whether he was some kind of divine being. The Buddha said no, he wasn't a divine being, he was an awakened being – a Buddha. The wanderer looked him up and down for a few minutes, then shrugged his shoulders, said 'Well, maybe....' and wandered off, rather symbolically, 'down a side track'.

But over the following years, countless people proved receptive to the Buddha's teaching. Following the awakening of the five ascetics, the number of the Buddha's awakened disciples increased rapidly. At a large gathering of them, the Buddha said 'There are those who will be lost through not hearing the teaching. Some will understand.' With this in mind, he sent them to wander in different directions 'for the welfare and happiness of many, out of compassion for the world'.[1] Before long, the Buddha's disciples gained numerous disciples of their own. In this way, directly or indirectly, during his own lifetime the Buddha enabled many hundreds of men and women to gain full awakening, and thousands to attain other degrees of insight. They included several members of his own family. Though he had to go forth from home in order to realize the truth, the Buddha wanted his family to have every opportunity to benefit from his realization. On his return he was greeted with resistance and suspicion by some members of his clan. His former wife responded to his arrival by telling their son, Rahula – who may have been eight or nine years old by this time – to ask his father for his inheritance. Quite how she expected the Buddha to respond to this can only be guessed at, but the result was possibly not what she had been expecting. Obediently chasing after the Buddha, Rahula cried 'Give me my inheritance! Give me my inheritance!' The Buddha, having long since given up his worldly possessions, had only one inheritance he could offer his son – the Dharma. Taking the boy at his word, he asked one of his chief disciples, Shariputra, to offer his son the 'going forth', meaning admission to the Buddha's order of renunciants as a novice. Looked after by Shariputra, Rahula remained in the order as a novice until, at the age of twenty, he became a full member. Shortly afterwards, whilst in conversation with his father, Rahula attained awakening.

Other members of the Buddha's family also came to be among his closest followers. Both his father and his foster-mother eventually attained awakening. His foster-mother, Mahaprajapati, was later instrumental in the Buddha's founding of an order of female renunciants dependent on alms, a development then without precedent in Indian religious culture. The Buddha's half-brother and a number of his cousins also followed his teaching and became renunciant mendicants. Among these was his cousin Ananda, who later became the Buddha's most faithful attendant and closest companion. Although of a similar age to the Buddha, Ananda outlived him by some decades and played a crucial role in consolidating the Buddha's teaching.

The earliest and most historically dependable records of the Buddha's life and teaching are contained in the Pali canon, a collection of texts preserved by the Theravada school of Buddhism. Although these texts are very formalized – partly as a result of having been passed down orally for several hundred years before they were finally committed to writing – details still emerge of the Buddha as a person, rather than as an icon.

As time went on, the Buddha became the focus of a great deal of attention. An increasing number of people followed his example and went forth from home to practise his teaching, often accompanying him on his travels. At the same time, his many householder followers were always keen to see him, receive his teachings, and – especially – to entertain him and his followers. It must have been a very demanding life, and even the Buddha needed at times to get away from it all. Though his awakened mind was completely beyond the possibility of self-oriented reactions such as irritation, his body was still subject to wear and tear. On one occasion, when the Buddha was staying near a major city, he found himself 'worried by monks and nuns, lay-followers, both men and women, by rajas and royal ministers, by sectarians and their followers.' So, without telling anyone, he walked off into the forest, where he remained for some time, alone except for a solitary bull-elephant which, 'worried by elephants and she-elephants and calf elephants and sucklings' had, according to the tale, similarly left the herd behind for some peace and quiet.[2]

It also emerges from the Pali canon that the Buddha was capable of making a mistake. This is illustrated by one occasion on which his teaching had serious unintended consequences. One of the subjects of meditation that the Buddha taught his renunciant disciples was the contemplation of loathsomeness, particularly the loathsome aspects of the human body. This meditation, which is still practised today, is a means of developing a sense of positive non-attachment to the body. However, it can only be effective if done on the basis of a very high level of esteem and well-wishing towards oneself. On one particular occasion, the Buddha taught this meditation to a group of monks and left them to practise it. On his return a few weeks later, he discovered that a number of them had committed suicide, having become 'humiliated, ashamed, and disgusted' with their bodies. Learning from this major calamity, the Buddha afterwards ensured that the contemplation of loathsomeness was taught only to those ready for such strong medicine.

Later Buddhist traditions – especially in their more popular manifestations – tended to treat the Buddha as an all-knowing, superhuman being. However, this incident, coming as it does from among the earliest Buddhist records, makes it clear that the Buddha was not omniscient in this way. According to tradition, the Buddha was omniscient in the sense that he knew everything about the path to awakening and the state of awakening itself. He was not omniscient in the sense of knowing what was going on in everyone's minds.

Apart from this incident, the Buddha's recorded teaching was always appropriate, well judged, and to the point. There are hundreds of episodes in the Pali canon that clearly demonstrate his deep understanding of people. These include the account of a non-Buddhist recluse named Bahiya the Bark Clad (probably a reference to an ascetic practice of wearing a garment made of tree bark), who lived on the west coast of India, a long way from the Buddha's area of activity. Bahiya was deeply devoted to his spiritual practice – as his name suggests, it probably involved austerities – and wondered whether he had yet attained awakening. A *deva* (heavenly being) appeared and told him that not only was he not awakened, but he was practising in a way that would never lead to awakening. But, said the deva, there was a person – the Buddha – living far off, who could teach him the way to awakening. Bahiya set out immediately and, except to eat and sleep, didn't stop walking until he reached where the Buddha was staying. The Buddha's followers told him that the Buddha was on his alms round, and that he would return shortly.

However, Bahiya could not wait. He found the Buddha and begged for a teaching straight away. The Buddha, who did not usually give teachings during his alms round, told Bahiya that it was not the proper time. 'Sir,' said Bahiya, 'one never knows how long life will last – yours or mine. Please give me your teaching.' Again the Buddha said that it was not the proper time, and again Bahiya repeated his plea. If anyone went so far as to ask the Buddha for something three times, he usually put his reservations to one side and let them have what they wanted. So the Buddha gave Bahiya a very pithy teaching: in essence, 'You must train yourself like this: in the seen, there is only the seen; in the heard, only the heard; in the imagined, only the imagined; and in the apprehended, only the apprehended.'

Having said this, the Buddha continued on his way. Just then, Bahiya's sense of urgency and the unpredictability of life was vindicated, as he was attacked and killed by a rampaging bullock. When news of this reached the Buddha, he asked his disciples to cremate Bahiya's body and build a ceremonial cairn over the remains, an honour reserved for exceptional people. The disciples were curious to know why Bahiya should be accorded this honour. The Buddha replied 'Monks, Bahiya the Bark Clad practised the teaching and has won complete liberation.'[3] In other words, Bahiya's ability to realize the full import of the Buddha's words straight away showed that he was exceptionally spiritually developed and worthy of special honour.

Another well-known incident from the ancient commentaries on the Pali canon shows the Buddha taking a very different approach. A young boy from the Buddha's own clan had died, and his mother – Kisa Gotami – was plunged into such inconsolable grief that she refused to accept his death. Instead, she carried the child's corpse from house to house, asking people for medicine that would cure him. Most people mocked her, but one man realized that her grief had made her temporarily insane. He told her there was only one person who might know the right medicine – the Buddha. Kisa Gotami went to the Buddha, still clutching the body of her son. 'You did well to come to me,' said the Buddha, 'Now go round the town and bring back to me some mustard seed from a house where nobody has died.'

With hope in her heart, Kisa Gotami started at the nearest house and asked the people living there whether they had any mustard seed. 'Yes indeed,' they replied. 'But,' she asked, 'I have to know, has anyone ever died here?' The people's faces became grave. 'Please, Gotami, do not remind us of our sorrow,' they replied. And a similar story emerged from every house she visited. After some time, she quietly went down to the cremation ground, left her son's corpse there, and returned to the Buddha. 'Have you got the mustard seed, Gotami?' the Buddha asked. 'Sir,' she replied 'the matter of the mustard seed is over. Now I know that I am not the only one to have suffered bereavement; death is the common lot of all human beings.' Having absorbed this insight into the human condition, she asked the Buddha to accept her as a disciple.

The Buddha's skill as a teacher enabled Kisa Gotami to learn for herself what she really needed to know. This was always his primary concern as a teacher – not to expect people to accept a set of predigested, stereotyped teachings, nor to persuade them to become his disciples, but simply to enable them to gain an ever clearer, immediate understanding of their own nature. He was active in this enterprise until almost the moment of his death. We will touch upon some of the concluding episodes from the Buddha's life later.

The Buddha's many remarkable qualities as an awakened human being and teacher could give the impression of someone who was entirely superhuman, even beyond our emulation. However, this would be to miss the point entirely – hence the importance of the Pali canon's evidence of the Buddha's essential humanity. He was awakened, yes, but he was an awakened *human being*. For us, perhaps the most important thing to remember about the Buddha – the Buddha-Jewel – is the point that this chapter started with: *every human being is a potential Buddha*. Each of us has the potential to become awakened. In the next chapter, we will begin to explore how we might go about achieving this.

2

APPROACHING THE DHARMA

THE MYSTERIOUS BLUE DEPTHS of the Dharma Jewel represent truth itself – the nature of things as they really are. But, from our unawakened perspective, we see not the depths but the sparkling, multi-faceted surface of the Jewel: the varied means – making up the way or path – which enable us to move towards awakening.

When we look more closely, we see that all these small facets help to make up two great principal facets of the Dharma Jewel: one consisting of all the teachings that express the truth, the other consisting of all the practices that enable progress towards the realization of that truth. Although the term 'Dharma' has various meanings and connotations, in Buddhist contexts it is to these two aspects – the teachings and practices – that it usually refers.

The Dharma in this sense began with the Buddha's own teaching, but it does not end there. It also encompasses the developments and refinements of later Buddhist traditions. The fact that the Dharma continued to be refined and developed after the time of the Buddha does not mean there was anything lacking in the Buddha's awakening or in his own teaching. The Buddha was fully awakened; but he was still one person with a limited lifespan. After his awakening, he had perhaps forty-five years left in which to develop his teaching and communicate his vision to others. This was simply not long enough for him to expound all the heights and depths of awakening.

The oldest records of Buddhism imply that the Buddha himself began this process of refining and developing the teachings. He was continually searching for new ways to communicate awakening to others, often in response to the needs of individual people and situations. In subsequent centuries, many of the Buddha's awakened successors discovered other ways of expressing new perspectives on the Dharma and new means to awakening. This is a process that will always continue. The map of the path to awakening has constantly to be redrawn to take into account the changing environment and the needs of society. Fortunately, the creativity of the awakened mind is limitless!

THE THREE LEVELS OF UNDERSTANDING

The rich variety of forms created to express aspects of the Dharma Jewel reflect its extraordinary depth and inexhaustible potential. How can we comprehend something so profound? In order to understand the Dharma, we have to approach it in the right way. This way is outlined in the three levels of understanding (or wisdom): learning, reflecting, and meditating. These three levels can be applied to any Dharma teaching or practice. To illustrate this, let's see how we could apply them to understanding the Buddhist teaching on impermanence.

THE THREE LEVELS OF UNDERSTANDING	
Learning	Clarification of meaning
Reflecting	Assimilation of meaning
Meditating	Direct apprehension of meaning

The First Level: Understanding Through Learning

When we first come across the teaching on impermanence, our initial objective is to ensure that we understand the word. It will almost certainly have implications and nuances for us already, but we cannot assume that these reflect the Buddhist teaching. We need to determine what impermanence implies in the Buddhist sense. And to do this, we have to examine what the Buddhist tradition has to say about it.

Originally, this learning process would have involved listening to teachings about the meaning of impermanence – hence this level is traditionally referred to as 'understanding through listening'. 'Listening' might suggest a passive approach, but this first level of understanding involves active learning – making a determined effort, without preconceptions, to understand what the tradition is saying in its own terms. This requires energy, patience, self-awareness, and even some courage, particularly in seeing through preconceptions that might undermine our understanding.

Preconceptions come in many forms. A common source is our cultural or religious conditioning. For example, someone may believe there *has* to be a supreme creator God somewhere in Buddhism, because all religions teach the existence of God. They may look for ways to incorporate or allow for the existence of God in Buddhism despite the Buddhist teachings – including that of impermanence – that quite clearly undermine such a notion.

Preconceptions also take the form of assumptions about the words used to translate Buddhist terms. For this reason, some translators consciously avoid using words that have misleading connotations. For example, one quality that Buddhists aspire to embody is often described as 'loving-kindness'. It could equally be described as 'love', but many Westerners understand this primarily as romantic or sexual love rather than the impartial and non-sexual love that the Buddhist term connotes.[4]

Preconceptions and assumptions should not, however, present much difficulty at this first level of understanding. Buddhist teachings have been successfully translated into many different languages and conveyed to people from very different cultures, and this difficulty always has to be overcome. What matters is that we are aware that we have preconceptions, and watch out for their effects.

As this suggests, at this first level of understanding we need to be able to think clearly, rationally, and objectively. Developing our thinking skills is an important requisite of the Buddhist path. People sometimes suppose that, because awakening cannot itself be expressed conceptually, clear and logical thought has no place in Buddhism. Such views seem to be confirmed by popular stories about Zen masters who burn or abuse Buddhist scriptures. However, in the original context, these stories would not have been intended or understood as a complete refutation of the use of words and concepts. The Zen masters may well have been pointing to the dangers of attachment to scriptures, words, and concepts when it is time to go beyond them. But it is not time to go beyond them when we have just started to understand them.

In practice, the Buddhist tradition uses words and concepts for all they are worth. When their worth has been transcended, it leaves them behind. However, this final going beyond only comes as the culmination of the third level of understanding.

The Second Level: Understanding Through Reflecting

At this level, we begin to reflect on impermanence in any of the many and varied ways recommended by the tradition. By reflecting on the teaching – both in formal meditation sessions and more generally – our understanding of it deepens. It becomes more and more genuinely meaningful, rather than, as it may have been at first, just an abstract idea. In this way, we are getting more of a *feeling* for impermanence. It is becoming an integral part of our outlook on life, even if still on a relatively superficial level. We have not yet fully realized its implications. At this level of understanding, then, we are deepening our exploration of the teaching and gradually assimilating it on both a rational and an emotional level. As a result of this, the next level of understanding will tend to arise.

The Third Level: Understanding Through Meditating

'Meditating' here specifically means the kind of meditation discovered by Siddhartha on the night of his awakening. It is not meditation in the sense of a technique or method, but meditation as an experience of insight. This would mean that our understanding of impermanence has ripened into a direct apprehension of all its implications. We would be seeing, directly and therefore beyond any possible doubt, that the teaching of impermanence really does point out the way in which all things exist.

Experiencing this level of understanding – or insight – does not, however, mean that we are now awakened. As we'll see later, cultivating and deepening this kind of insight continues throughout a Buddhist's whole life – perhaps throughout many lives.

Rather paradoxically, perhaps, the more we consolidate understanding through meditating, the more we will be able to develop insight into impermanence under any circumstances, and not just in the context of formal meditation sessions. Ultimately this is the way to the realization of wisdom in the full sense – the teachings become so closely enwoven with our consciousness that they become part of the fabric of our being, and we fully and finally see through our delusion. To use a traditional analogy, the mixing of our consciousness and insight into impermanence would be just like 'water being mixed with water'. Only an awakened person embodies this fully.

THE RELATIONSHIP BETWEEN TEACHING AND PRACTICE

Having seen how to approach the Dharma, we can move on to a broader picture of the Dharma itself. As we saw at the start of this chapter, the Dharma Jewel has two dimensions. Its inner dimension is awakening itself – the truth, which is realization of the way things really are. As the teaching of the three levels of understanding makes clear, we cannot realize this truth right away. We can only approach it by way of the multi-faceted outer dimension of the Dharma Jewel: all the teachings which the Buddhist tradition uses to point to the way things really are, and all the practices or methods of self-transformation that lead towards awakening.

Although teachings and practices may at first appear to be two different things, the further we proceed with them through the levels of understanding, the less distinction there is between them. For instance, we may begin by reading about Buddhism, and at the same time take up the practice of meditation. At first these seem to be two quite different kinds of activity. However, when we are ready to approach some aspect of Buddhist teaching at the second level of understanding, and begin to reflect on it in our meditation, the boundary between teaching and practice starts to break down. Then, both our meditation and our penetration into the doctrinal aspects of the Dharma deepen together. Finally, with the arising of insight, our theoretical understanding is united perfectly with our daily practice. We are no longer treading the path because we have become one with the path – and the goal.

To begin this process, however, we need to understand the principle of the path.

THE DYNAMIC OF THE PATH

It is sometimes said that there are as many different paths to awakening as there are individuals who aspire to become awakened. In one sense, at least, this is true. Just as the route we take on a journey depends very much on where we start, so each person has a unique starting point – that is, each person starts with their own particular dispositions and conditionings, their own virtues and vices. It is in this sense that each person has to tread a path that is different from anyone else's.

This is, incidentally, one of the reasons Buddhism considers it so important to have direct contact with spiritual teachers and friends. Although books can give us an idea of how to practise Buddhism, our unique qualities mean that, sooner or later, we'll get into our own unique difficulties. When this happens, a teacher or friend (best of all, a teacher who is a friend) who knows us well, and who knows the Dharma well, is invaluable in helping us to see the next step. Nevertheless, teachers and friends cannot tread the path for us. They can point us in the right direction, but the journey can only be made by ourselves.

As the need for such teachers and friends suggests, the fact that we each have to tread our own path does not mean that we simply invent the path as we go along. There are two aspects to the path – what we might call its 'geography' and its 'dynamic'. It is the geography of the path that is unique for each individual; its dynamic, on the other hand, is broadly the same for everyone. An image may help to clarify this.

Imagine a lofty snow-capped mountain, rising from dense jungle-clad terrain on a large island in the middle of a vast ocean. People wishing to climb the mountain must first reach the island, each approaching it from a different direction. Currents and tides ensure that no two people ever land in the same place. When they land, although the peak is not yet visible, they set off in what they think is the right direction, battle their way through dense jungle and across rivers, and cope as best they can with the local wildlife. Eventually, they realize that the ground is rising and that at last they are on the lower slopes of the mountain itself. The vegetation thins out, bare rock shows through, the sun beats down on them, water is scarce. Sooner or later, they are climbing upon rock, then gingerly crossing glaciers towards an ice-clad ridge that rises to the cloud-hidden summit. After much hardship and danger the mountain is climbed, and the summit reached.

This scenario has its limitations as a metaphor for the path to awakening, and should not be taken too literally. (After all, with real mountains, we have to climb down again!) But it does show the sense in which the *geography* of the journey will be unique for each individual: the particular landing point, path through the jungle, wild animals encountered, and approach to the summit. Each route has its own degree of difficulty, its own kinds of challenge. On the other hand, each explorer will encounter more or less similar experiences, in more or less the same order: ocean, jungle, peak. In this sense we can see how the *dynamic* of the way to the mountain summit is broadly the same.

It is this dynamic of progress towards awakening that is reflected in the different versions of the Buddhist path, although some give more 'geographical' details than others (in any case, the geography and dynamic are obviously very closely related). A number of these paths are very well known and widely taught and practised in Buddhist traditions, while others are less well known. In order to get a clearer idea of the essential dynamic of the path, we will now look at a few of those paths in outline.

The Eightfold Path

The 'noble eightfold path' is one of the most important and best-known outlines of the way to awakening. It appears, together with the four truths, in records of the Buddha's very first teaching. It seems likely, though, that it was developed by the Buddha over a number of years. It begins with 'right view', which means developing clarity about the essential Dharma teachings, at least at the first two levels of understanding ('learning' and 'reflecting'). Also essential to right view, if it is understood in a fuller sense, is the development of some degree of feeling for, or vision of, awakening itself, however faint and remote this may be. This deepens our conviction that awakening is our ultimate potential as a human being.

The second stage of the eightfold path is the immediate practical corollary of this: 'right motivation'. If we are to move towards awakening, we need to transform our initial understanding into action, and we act effectively only when we are motivated. So the second stage involves developing and deepening our emotional engagement with the path. To do this, we need to be clear about our motives: for example, are we practising meditation because we are set upon awakening, or because we are looking for peace of mind, or because we just want a bit of peace and quiet?

While there is nothing wrong with the last two motives, they have nothing to do with the path to awakening as such. That said, our motives change; although some people take up Buddhist practices with awakening as their motive, others have different hopes and expectations, but find that their motives are developed and transformed through their deepening understanding of the path.

THE EIGHTFOLD PATH	
Right view	Developing clarity about the essential Dharma teachings; having some feeling for, or vision of, awakening itself
Right motivation	Developing and deepening emotional engagement in the path; clarity about motives
Right speech	Ways of putting the Dharma into action in everyday life
Right action	
Right livelihood	
Right effort	Ways of practising the Dharma inwardly
Right mindfulness	
Right samadhi	A meditative state that penetrates to the true nature of things

The following five stages do not have to be developed in the order in which they are usually listed. They represent qualities that need to be developed more or less simultaneously. Three of them – 'right speech', 'right action', and 'right livelihood' – cover ways in which we can put the Dharma into action in our everyday life. The next two – 'right effort' and 'right mindfulness' – deal mainly with ways in which we practise the Dharma inwardly. We will be looking at these five aspects more fully in the following chapters.

Finally, there is the stage of *samadhi*, a Sanskrit word usually translated in this context as 'right concentration', although this can be rather misleading. Like the word *dharma*, it is a many-layered term. As a stage in the eightfold path, it means a meditative state that penetrates to the true nature of things: in other words, it is a synonym for awakening.

A Five-Stage Path

Another, less well-known version of the path is found in a text called the *Meghiya Sutta*, from the Pali canon. In this text, the Buddha teaches a path with five stages that leads to the 'heart's release' – an apt and moving synonym for the state of awakening.

The Buddha describes the first stage of this path as the development of 'a lovely intimacy, a lovely friendship, a lovely comradeship'.

As we have just seen, without good friends, most people would not be able to sustain their progress on the path, or even begin the demanding task of transforming themselves. The second stage is the development of virtue: we strive to be 'restrained with the restraint of the obligations' (that is, the ethical precepts) and 'perfect in the practice of right behaviour'. Thirdly, there is 'talk that is serious and suitable for opening up the heart and which conduces to dispassion, calm, comprehension, perfect insight, nirvana'. This means study and comprehension of the Dharma itself as the path to awakening. Fourthly, we live 'resolute in energy for the abandoning of unprofitable things, for the acquiring of profitable things'. In the broadest sense, this is the practice of meditation, including meditation extended into daily life in the form of mindfulness or awareness. Finally, we become 'endowed with the insight that goes on to penetrate the perfect ending of suffering'.

The Six Perfections

Another version of the path that is very important in the Mahayana (see Chapter 9) or 'Great Way' schools of Buddhism is known as the 'six perfections' or 'six transcendental virtues'. This path begins with the practice of generosity. The five succeeding stages are ethical behaviour (or skilful action), patience and forbearance, energy and vigour, meditation, and wisdom, which is tantamount to awakening itself.

The Common Dynamic Structure

These outlines of the Buddhist path clearly have features or stages in common, but can we detect in them any shared underlying dynamic? To guide us, there is another path, known as the 'three trainings' or 'threefold path'. This encapsulates the common dynamic structure that underlies not only the paths outlined above but all possible versions of the path to awakening. Its three elements are each paths or ways in themselves: they are the way of skilful (or ethical) action, the way of meditation, and the way of wisdom. On this path, the stages are successive: the first path leads to the second, and the second to the third – although, as we will see, we will need to progress through the threefold sequence more than once.

We can apply this threefold analysis to all versions of the path in Buddhist scriptural sources. For example, in the *Meghiya Sutta's* five-stage path, the way of skilful action is formulated as the practice of virtuous conduct and right behaviour; in the six perfections, it is formulated as generosity, ethics, patience, and vigour; and in the noble eightfold path it is formulated as right speech, right action, and right livelihood. Similarly, each of these paths has elements covering the way of meditation and the way of wisdom.

As the three trainings represent the fundamental dynamic of the path to awakening, it is in terms of skilful action, meditation, and wisdom that we will explore the Dharma in the following chapters.

3

THE WAY OF SKILFUL ACTION

THE THREE TRAININGS – skilful action, meditation, and wisdom – have a sequential relationship: skilful action is the basis for meditation, and meditation is the basis for wisdom. This does not mean, however, that we practise each one separately, spending years on nothing but skilful action, then more years just meditating, before finally we are ready to start on wisdom. Each stage is practised not once but many times, and the dynamic of spiritual development involves progressing through all three stages again and again, at ever higher levels. The three stages are therefore inextricably linked. How and why they interconnect becomes clearer if we look at each stage in terms of how we develop *skilful mental states*. First, though, we need to understand just what the terms 'skilful' and 'unskilful' mean in their Buddhist context.

SKILFUL AND UNSKILFUL

Developing skilful mental states – and preventing the development of unskilful ones – is central to the path to awakening. To a large extent the terms speak for themselves. If we were using them in the ordinary sense, we might describe someone as a 'skilful' potter if they produce attractive teapots that pour well, or as an 'unskilful' potter if they produce hideous ones that drip. Just as potters create out of the raw materials available to them, so we all create our own lives and characters out of the raw material we are born with, and we can go about this in skilful or unskilful ways. At any given moment in our lives, we have the capacity to act either skilfully or unskilfully.

'Skilful' is a fairly literal translation of a word that also has connotations of 'clever, expert, right, meritorious' and even 'beautiful'. 'Unskilful' has the opposite connotations. So what is it that makes a skilful act skilful, or an unskilful one unskilful? From the Buddhist point of view, it is not enough to say that something is skilful because it is 'good' or unskilful because it is 'bad', because that still begs the question.

Broadly speaking, actions are unskilful to the extent that they arise from mental states of craving, aversion, and delusion; and skilful to the extent that they arise from mental states of non-craving, non-aversion, and non-delusion. As we have seen, self-centred acts arise from our basic delusion, typically expressed in craving and aversion. Craving, aversion, and delusion are known as the 'unskilful roots', because *all* unskilful mental states and actions grow from them. Unselfish or selfless mental states and acts, on the other hand, arise from the corresponding 'skilful roots' of generosity, kindness, and intelligent awareness or wisdom.

All the teachings, methods, and practices that make up the Dharma aim to help human beings realize awakening through the cultivation and consolidation of ever more skilful states of mind. The term 'mental states' or 'mind' in Buddhism encompasses all the mental functions, such as thinking, perception, awareness, intention, feeling, and emotion. Mental states comprise what happens not only on the conscious level of our mind but also on the subconscious and super-conscious (meditative) levels.

SKILFUL MENTAL STATES IN THE THREE TRAININGS

We can now look at how each of the three trainings embodies a specific kind or level of skilfulness. The first of the trainings, the way of skilful action, is concerned mainly with our relations with other people and the world. In terms of cultivating skilful mental states, it involves stopping or eradicating behaviour that is not skilfully motivated, and learning to act more and more from motives of generosity, kindness, and awareness.

When the path has been fully realized, the mind of an awakened person will be just as skilful in activity as it is in meditation. This is not the case when we are nearer to the beginning of the path; because the way of action is mainly concerned with our activity in the world at large – with all its distractions, pressures, and demands – it is likely at first to be something of a bumpy ride. At first, most people find it relatively easier to cultivate skilful mental states in their meditation. However, the real challenge lies in expressing and maintaining skilful mental states in relation to other people.

THE THREE TRAININGS	
The way of skilful action	Cultivating actions that are skilfully motivated
The way of meditation	Cultivating continuous streams of skilful mental states
The way of wisdom	Cultivating a continuous and irreversible stream of skilful mental states

Nevertheless, acting as skilfully as possible is indispensable as the basis for meditation. It is indispensable because our efforts to cultivate skilful states in our everyday lives will make it easier for us to cultivate similar but more subtle skilful states in meditation. If we are not making an effort to be more skilful in our everyday lives, our meditation practice is unlikely to develop.

The second training, the way of meditation, involves the cultivation of a continuous stream of skilful mental states. The main difference between the way of meditation and the way of action is that in meditation we are developing skilfulness within mental states themselves. In other words, we are developing skilful responses to our own mental events rather than to the stimulus of external events. At the same time, the more we cultivate skilful mental states through meditation, the more they will find expression through our actions. In this way, skilful action and meditation increase each other's effectiveness. Skilful action prepares us for meditation, while meditation feeds increasingly skilful states back into everyday action.

But there is a problem inherent in meditation. Although we can develop a continuous stream of skilful mental states, these states continue only while we are meditating. Once we stop, less skilful mental states arise. For example, we might start the day by practising the development of loving-kindness (see page 77), and genuinely feel love and goodwill towards all living beings. But if we then walk into the living room and find our children daubing paint on the wall, our loving-kindness is likely to dissipate rather quickly!

If we had developed wisdom, our loving-kindness would not even waver, and anger would not arise, because, once wisdom is fully developed, skilful mental states are not only continuous but *irreversible*. Our response to a spoiled wall (or much worse) could no longer be anger, because anger is an expression of delusion – and once wisdom is fully developed, delusion is no longer present.

This does not mean that wisdom involves merely fatalistic acceptance of whatever happens. There is no contradiction between wisdom and teaching our children a sense of care and responsibility – quite the reverse. A bit of judicious shouting may even be appropriate in some circumstances, but this response would be prompted by concern and kindness rather than by irritation, anger, or the desire for reprisal.

Such unwaveringly skilful responses are the mark of someone who is fully awakened, or well on the way to awakening. Wisdom has to be developed, and much of the way of meditation is, in effect, this development. The development of a continuous stream of skilful mental states is only the first element of meditation; we need to put these skilful mental states into the service – so to speak – of the development of insight.

The development of insight means, as we have seen, an ever clearer perspective on the way things really are. Buddhists often speak of 'insight *meditation*', but the further we proceed with the three ways of action, meditation, and wisdom, the more the development of insight or wisdom will imbue the whole of our lives – to the point where we are able to use any situation to deepen our insight. Having reached this point, it could be said that we have entered the way of wisdom proper.

In practice, each of the three trainings is constantly interrelating with the others, in a way unique to each individual. Generally speaking, we can practise each training at each of the three levels of understanding. So, for example, we could start by reading about skilful action in order to clarify it. This would be equivalent to understanding through learning. Then we would be in a position to review our actions and consider putting our understanding into practice – equivalent to understanding through reflecting. Eventually we would act skilfully because this had become the natural expression of our mental states – equivalent to understanding through meditating.

However, real life is not likely to be as neat and systematic as this – and if you were to ask a Buddhist which of the three trainings he or she was currently practising and at which level of understanding, you'd be as likely to get a blank look as a clear answer. Bearing this in mind, let's now get to grips with at least the first level of understanding of the first of the three trainings, the way of skilful action.

BUDDHIST ETHICS

As we have seen, the distinction between skilful and unskilful is the basis of the Buddhist approach to ethics. What makes our actions skilful or unskilful is not, essentially, the nature of the act itself, but the motivation underlying the act – the mental state from which the act arises.

This runs counter to many Western assumptions about ethics, which are strongly influenced by the very different Judaeo-Christian approach. In the monotheistic religions the arbiter of morality and universal law-giver is God. As noted in the Introduction, many people in the West, even those with no particular religious allegiance, seem to find it difficult to imagine human beings behaving ethically without God being there in the background. Without God-given absolutes of right and wrong, they suggest, there would be no reason to behave ethically.

Buddhism does not depend on a God in order to explain or justify ethical action. What is skilful or unskilful is not imposed upon us from outside, but determined by the very structure of our consciousness with its potential for both self-centred and selfless action. Buddhist ethics are based on the principle that as we choose to act, so we become. Skilful actions, by their very nature, lead to happier, brighter states, while unskilful actions, by their very nature, lead to the opposite. The more that we act out of generosity, kindness, and awareness, the more those qualities become part of what we are, and the more spontaneously we will continue to express them. On the other hand, the more we act out of craving and aversion, the more these unskilful qualities will dominate our consciousness and find expression in our actions. We have no need of an external agency to punish or reward our actions.

In Buddhist terms, truly ethical action involves responding fully and appropriately to all the situations we come across. To take such responsibility, we need a clear understanding of the ethical implications of any situation. We are constantly presented with choices, often in very minor ways, between skilful and unskilful courses of action. Do we tell a small white lie to get out of an awkward situation, or admit the truth? Do we remember to repay a small amount of money that we borrowed, or conveniently forget it? Do we allow ourselves to snap at an innocent colleague when we are feeling irritable, or acknowledge but contain our feelings?

In our daily lives, then, it is very important to be able to distinguish skilful from unskilful action. Not surprisingly, there is no simple list of skilful and unskilful actions. It is possible for the same action to be either skilful or unskilful, because what matters is the underlying motivation. For example, giving a present to somebody could be a simple expression of kindness, appreciation, or generosity, and hence skilful – or it could be an unskilful attempt to manipulate them.

Similarly, we need to be aware of our motives for refraining from overtly wrong actions. For example, we may hold back from murdering the boss only because we fear getting punished for it – a reluctant compliance with authoritarian morality. A more skilful motive would be our understanding that, however justified we felt in our murderous feelings, it would be an exceedingly unskilful act, rooted in aversion. At the highest level of ethical practice, when our mental states and actions are entirely skilful, such a plan or fantasy would never enter our mind, however badly the boss was treating us.

Not all situations are as clear-cut, of course, and it is sometimes impossible to see clearly what is the skilful and what the unskilful option. Deciding on the most skilful course of action has to be a matter of using whatever qualities of intelligence, awareness, and insight we have developed so far, in order to arrive at the best decision. Most importantly, we have to take responsibility for the consequences of our actions – all our actions, whether they are skilful or unskilful.

In principle, ethical action requires nothing more than an understanding of what is skilful and what is unskilful, and sufficient awareness to apply this knowledge to the circumstances of our life. However, 'sufficient' here means 'a lot' – a much higher and more consistent level of awareness than most people are likely to have when making their first tentative efforts with the three trainings.

In order to support the practice of skilful action in daily life, the Buddhist tradition has evolved many different kinds of practical guidelines, or precepts. These highlight the main areas of life in which we need to develop greater awareness of our skilful and unskilful motivations. They should not be approached as lists of commandments; nor should they be regarded as embodying the right action in all possible circumstances. Rather, we should take them as training principles that help us to develop skilfulness in action.

There are many lists of precepts in different Buddhist traditions, some very long, some quite short. The most basic, and most widely practised, is a set of five precepts which almost certainly go back to the time of the Buddha himself. Attempting to follow these five precepts represents the basis of Buddhist ethical practice – and doing so effectively amounts to following the way of skilful action. Like all Buddhist practices, they are demanding – to follow them we have to change our life. To see what the way of skilful action demands of us, we will take a look at each of them in turn.

THE FIVE PRECEPTS

Each of these precepts has two aspects: one activity that is to be developed and one that is to be avoided.

THE FIVE PRECEPTS	
Negative aspect	**Positive aspect**
1 To abstain from causing injury to living beings	Kindness
2 To abstain from taking that which is not given	Generosity
3 To abstain from sexual misconduct	Contentment
4 To abstain from untruthful speech	Truthfulness
5 To abstain from intoxicants	Mindfulness

Kindness; and Abstention From Causing Injury to Living Beings

The first precept involves cultivating and expressing kindness, love, and compassion towards others; and abstaining from acts which directly or indirectly cause injury to living beings. Non-injury is the most basic and indispensable of Buddhist ethical principles. To harm a fellow living being, and particularly to inflict death, is doing to another what we would least like done to ourselves.

The kinds of unskilful motives that underlie the injuring or killing of others can derive from any (or all) of the three unskilful roots of craving, aversion, and delusion. Violence is most obviously sparked off by aversion-led emotions such as anger and hatred, but they are also fuelled by craving-led emotions like greed, covetousness, and jealousy. The motivations that lead to violence can be very complex, with craving-led and aversion-led emotions inciting and exacerbating each other.

On the collective level, war and aggressive imperialism (of both cultural and military varieties) are motivated by the same kinds of unskilful emotion complexes that underlie individual violence. In such cases the nation state, or the ethnic, religious, or political group, acts in the same way as an individual ego-identity. Perhaps it craves dominion, power, and influence; or it wants to exterminate ethnic, religious, or political groups that it regards as threatening. From a Buddhist point of view, it is impossible to reconcile a state's justification, let alone glorification, of violence and murder in war with its punishment of the same behaviour at an individual level. Both represent the most deeply unskilful behaviour.

For those caught up in such situations, the motivation for killing might not be fanaticism or hatred so much as bewilderment and a tendency to go along with the collective will. Or it may be fear of disapproval or punishment, or fear of one's own death, together with a lack of sufficient motivation to resist the command to kill. And often – as seems to have been the case with many ordinary soldiers in the First World War – it is for reasons that the individual is quite unable to understand.

It may appear from this that a Buddhist must, in all circumstances, turn the other cheek and be an absolute pacifist, but this is not necessarily the case. For a Buddhist, aggression would seem to be out of the question. But what if we are a victim of aggression? Should we do nothing?

There are no pat answers to such questions. Buddhist ethics demand personal responsibility. If we find ourselves in a war or some other serious conflict, there is no choice but to respond – an attempt to ignore the situation would just be a denial of responsibility. It may be that constructive and humanitarian responses are possible without becoming a combatant. On the other hand, when the communist Chinese invaded Tibet in 1950, many Buddhist Tibetans did take up arms to resist them. Had they succeeded in forcing the Chinese back, the human, cultural, and religious genocide that subsequently took place in Tibet might have been avoided. Were these people right or wrong to try to defend all that was important to them by taking up arms? Each individual must make a choice, take responsibility for that choice, and be prepared to accept the consequences.

Deliberate killing is unskilful in any circumstances. No doubt many of the Chinese involved in the invasion and occupation of Tibet were themselves victims of coercion, acting out of fear and bewilderment. They too had families, lovers, parents, children, friends, their own dreams, wishes, and aspirations – their own humanity. As soon as we start to conceive of someone as 'the enemy' we lose sight of their humanity – empathy and compassion go out of the window, and this diminishes our own humanity. If we do decide, taking all things into consideration, that we should fight, then we must do so in full knowledge of the very high price that will be paid.

The ethical questions involved in the individual's response to such situations are extremely complex, and this discussion broaches only some of the more basic issues. However, there are other less complicated choices in our lives where the first precept offers us clear guidance. For many Buddhists, their choice of diet is one, and a practical expression of the first precept is vegetarianism. 'Food' animals, particularly those raised by modern factory-farming methods, experience various kinds of suffering and distress, or at the very least are prematurely put to death. If we are trying to develop an ever fuller expression of kindness towards all living beings, this is inconsistent with our participation in such suffering and killing – even if our involvement is as remote as buying a frozen pastrami pizza.

As with all the precepts, each of us has to decide how we can put the principle into practice according to our own circumstances. There may be several difficulties to overcome before we can be completely vegetarian, and a gradual reduction in meat eating could be regarded as a commitment to following this precept.

Not all Buddhists are vegetarians, especially in some parts of the world where Buddhism has long been part of the culture. There is no simple explanation for this. On one level, people who live in places where it is genuinely impossible to survive as a vegetarian can and do observe the spirit of the precept by eating as few animals as possible. Some Buddhists even argue against vegetarianism. Often, however, Buddhists eat meat because of a literalistic understanding of the precept: 'I should not kill an animal myself, but it is all right if there is a non-Buddhist butcher nearby to do it for me.' Literalism of this kind completely undermines the Buddhist ethic of awareness and personal responsibility.

Physical harm is not the only kind of injury we can cause, either intentionally or indirectly: acts of coercion, manipulation, or exploitation may leave no marks on the bodies of their victims, but they are nonetheless an infliction of harm. Indulging an uncontrolled bad temper or aggressive and angry speech at the expense of our family, friends, colleagues, or strangers is also an act of violence. Here, following the principle of non-injury means trying to avoid the expression of unskilful emotions such as anger.

Avoiding the expression of such emotions is not the same as denying or repressing them. By the very nature of our unawakened state, we will inevitably feel anger and other unskilful emotions at times. There is absolutely nothing to be gained by pretending to ourselves that we are all sweetness and light. People often deny and repress negative emotions because of fear, pride, or a deluded belief that this is what being 'spiritual' requires. But if we habitually repress our 'unacceptable' emotions, the result, at best, is a kind of weak, passive 'niceness' with not-at-all-nice undertones. At worst, it is the stuff of psychotic disorder.

The Buddhist approach to dealing with strong negative emotion is to take the middle way: experience the emotion, but do not express it. For example, if anger arises you know you are angry, you know why you are angry, you can even say 'I'm getting very angry indeed about this,' but you do not start slamming doors, shouting, or throwing vases about the room. Rages of this sort might feel very satisfying in the short term, but they obviously have undesirable consequences. Apart from the fact that we are inflicting misery and harm on others, indulging anger only reinforces our tendency to become angry. Tantrums are rightly regarded as childish – a deeply immature, egocentric, and manipulative way of relating to others. So, too, are the withdrawal of affection, niggling criticism, and the various more covert ways in which people express their anger.

Some people argue that anger is justified, and perhaps even necessary, in the face of injustice, oppression, and suffering. Anger is undoubtedly a very natural response to injustice, and it may seem to provide the energy and motivation necessary to tackle a situation. But anger is, in itself, a strongly unskilful emotion. In a state of anger, our awareness is narrowed by powerful emotional turbulence and a strong desire to injure or destroy the object of our rage – which is why anger-led responses to oppression or injustice are all too likely to result in further oppression or injustice. Anger is a powerful fuel for social action – but a dangerous one.

The Buddha gave his analysis of this kind of situation unequivocally: 'Enmity is never appeased by enmity, only by friendliness; this is always the truth.'[5] Friendliness may at first seem an inadequate response to the darker aspects of human nature, and it makes huge demands on our courage and trust in humanity. But refusing to add yet more anger and hatred to a situation, and countering them instead with skilful positive emotions such as friendliness, kindness, love, and compassion, is the only way to a genuine, human, and humane resolution.

Of course, it is difficult enough to be friendly and kind to someone who merely irritates us, let alone to someone who seems to be set on causing harm. While strong feelings of friendliness, kindness, and love sometimes arise in us spontaneously, this is not enough: we need to develop them consciously, which requires a great deal of effort. We have already alluded to the very important Buddhist meditation for cultivating unlimited love and kindness, and we will be looking at this more closely in the next chapter. But even if, at any given time, we feel unable to respond to others with a genuine sense of kindness and concern for their well-being, we can at least try to be patient with them and abstain from harming them.

Each of the five precepts encourages us to abstain from behaviour that causes harm. The other four, in effect, work out the implications of non-injury in different areas of our lives.

Generosity; and Abstention From Taking That Which is Not Given

In essence, the second precept is about being generous in our relations with others. The negative counterpart of generosity, 'taking the not-given', is unskilful in that it arises from craving. It causes harm because it means taking from others things they do not wish to give up. 'The *not-given*' indicates that this means much more than simply abstaining from theft. What is not-given includes anything that another being does not wish us to take. If we are like Coleridge's Ancient Mariner, who could not stop himself fixing people with his 'glittering eye' and telling them of his life at great length whether they liked it or not, we are taking the not-given – demanding people's time and attention without their consent.

In the same way, we can presume on another's good will, patience, energy, liberality, or whatever other quality they possess which we want to exploit or draw on. It is very easy to do this without realizing it, especially with people we are very close to, so this precept calls for a lot of awareness.

As with all the precepts, avoiding harmful behaviour is merely the bottom line: the full expression of this precept is the positive quality of generosity. This means being prepared to be generous with all the things and qualities that we have: to be kind, concerned, and helpful, to be a good neighbour, to listen, to give of our own experience – the list could be very long indeed. It includes generosity in the more usual, material sense, especially the ability to give spontaneously. Giving money to charity is a valid and important expression of generosity – as is giving to buskers and beggars. It can sometimes be quite instructive to observe our rationalizations for not giving to beggars: 'They'll only spend it on drink,' 'It must be their own fault they're like that,' 'They probably make more money than I do.'... But giving unconditionally – if sensibly – can be very instructive too.

In generosity, as in all aspects of the way of skilful action, we need to be aware of our motivation. The giving of birthday, Christmas, or wedding presents sometimes degenerates into an empty ritual of mutual expectations rather than a genuine expression of generosity. And generosity does not mean allowing oneself to become a victim; other people may sometimes put unreasonable demands on our time, resources, or energy when it is neither appropriate nor possible for us to give it freely. If this happens, the most generous thing to do would be to ask them to stop it.

Contentment; and Abstention From Sexual Misconduct
Buddhism takes a pragmatic approach to sex. The sex drive is part of what we are. As far as Buddhist ethical teachings are concerned, sex can be enjoyed, whether for procreation or simply for pleasure, without any sense of guilt, furtiveness, or 'sinfulness'. It is fine to have a healthy sexual appetite – as long as it remains healthy.

'Sexual misconduct' means primarily any combination of sexual activity with elements of violence or gross exploitation. The sex drive is such a strong instinctive force in human beings that it easily by-passes the higher, rational and ethical parts of our psyche altogether. It can lead us into all sorts of unskilful, difficult, unpleasant and painful situations. The most extreme form of sexual unskilfulness is rape and, more indirectly, the infliction of physical injury or murder because of sexual obsession or jealousy.

Adultery is also very unskilful. By allowing our desire to take control it creates fear and deceit. Whether or not the deceived partner discovers the affair, acts of infidelity will certainly affect the degree of trust, intimacy, and commitment between partners. The defining factor of adultery is sexual deceit – it is irrelevant whether the two people are formally married, living together, or simply in an established sexual relationship.

Because sex is such a powerful drive, it needs to be kept in proportion. Many people relate to sex and sexual relationships as the chief source of satisfaction, security, and even of meaning in their lives. In one way or another it occupies most of their time, energy, and interest. This is a considerable over-investment in sex – not least because the Holy Grail of sexual fulfilment is hard to find and even harder to retain. So why is it that, despite the frustrations and personal risks involved, sex is such a preoccupation for so many people? In one sense, of course, it always has been and always will be: we have a inbuilt predisposition to propagate. However, the increasing emphasis on sexual fulfilment in Western society has paralleled a general decline in acceptance of traditional religious values. Could these two trends be connected? At least in part, the obsession with sexual fulfilment may have become a substitute for the sense of meaning that was once provided by religion.

Our sex drive cannot be healthy if we are over-investing in it. Over-investment means that sex and sexual relationships are used to compensate for lacks in other areas of our life – areas which may remain unexplored or underdeveloped as a result; and the value placed on sex opens the door to further unskilful situations such as adultery and manipulativeness within sexual relationships.

The positive expression of this precept, the development of contentment in relation to sex, is very important. At the most basic level, the practice of contentment means making a conscious effort to be satisfied with our existing sexual relationship – or absence of one – rather than dwelling on areas of dissatisfaction or fantasizing about other sexual partners.

If our strongest experiences of satisfaction and pleasure have invariably been derived from sexual activity, it can be difficult to imagine contentment in other than negative terms – absence of sex: absence of pleasure. However, contentment is a deeply satisfying experience in its own right. Far from being mere suppression of sexual feeling, it is a vibrantly positive experience of open, spacious, and intensely enjoyable mental states. For this reason, times of complete freedom from sexual activity are both valuable and desirable.

Of course, nobody literally engages in sexual activity all the time; but it is not unusual for sexual or sex-related thoughts, fantasies, and impulses to occupy a significant proportion of our mental space, often in such a habitual and semi-conscious way that we are hardly aware of it. This consumes a great deal of mental and emotional energy that could otherwise be directed towards developing deeper levels of contentment.

Innumerable Buddhists through the ages have practised celibacy – complete abstention from sexual activity – for part or most of their lives, in order to counter these deeply-ingrained tendencies and develop contentment. Many Buddhists today find that meditation retreats offer the best circumstances in which to experience deeper levels of contentment. Meditative states are by their nature states of contentment, and in the supportive circumstances of a retreat thoughts about sex diminish or cease altogether. At the very least, greater awareness of our mental states whilst on retreat can include greater awareness of how much we are driven by sexual impulses, giving us the opportunity to practise skilful ways of dealing with them. In meditative states, the gross sexual level of our experience is sublimated into much subtler and more deeply satisfying experiences – a sense of inner wholeness accompanied by joy, bliss, and concentration. As you might suppose from this, the development of contentment as an aspect of the way of skilful action is crucial as preparation for the way of meditation.

Finally, although the negative formulation of this precept focuses on sex, there are other aspects of our experience that can also arouse compulsive, craving-led behaviour – eating, working, taking physical risks, even meditation if it is driven by desire for heightened experiences. As we have seen, Buddhism identifies craving as one of the three roots of all unskilful action, so it is not surprising that it finds many different expressions. Whatever form the craving takes, the development of contentment, rather than the use of guilt or self-hatred to counteract our unskilful urges, is the response recommended by the third precept.

Truthfulness; and Abstention From Untruthful Speech

Speech is very much an outward expression of our mental and emotional states, skilful and unskilful. Much of our casual talk and banter is accompanied by very little awareness. It is mere verbalization rather than meaningful communication with other people. Usually the content of our more mindless chatter is relatively harmless, but it is precisely because we indulge in it with so little awareness that it can slip into less skilful speech: coarseness, gossip, stirring other people up or making digs at them disguised as humour.

From here, speech can degenerate into overtly unskilful expressions: anger, hostility, resentment, malice, and so forth. Words used in this way often incite physical violence, but they are also, as we have seen, instruments of violence in their own right, hence the importance of being able to recognize and act on the ethical implications of our speech.

Clearly these forms of unskilful speech have wider implications than simply truthfulness or untruthfulness. Another list of precepts adds a further three relating to speech: abstention from harsh, useless, and divisive speech, or in their positive aspect the development of kind, helpful, and harmonious speech. 'Right speech' does need to be developed in all possible ways; but, as with the other precepts, there is a bottom line, a minimum practical expression of the precept, and this is the avoidance of untruthful speech.

The main reason we use untruthful speech is to get our own way, or to get what we want. In this respect dishonest speech is self-centred speech; the essential motivation behind it is craving. Untruthful speech does not necessarily, or even usually, take the form of out-and-out lying. Many people regard blatant lies as unacceptable, but have far less compunction about using half-truths, white lies, or exaggeration and diminution of the facts in order to get what they want. It is in these areas that we need to do much of the work involved in practising the fourth precept. We need to develop awareness of our motivation for speaking as we do – which in turn requires honesty and self-knowledge.

Basic honesty is essential for real communication between people. To communicate meaningfully, we need to be aware of each other as individual human beings; but relating to another person dishonestly, in order to achieve what we desire, is relating to them as an object rather than as a person. This is why skilful communication starts with being as honest and truthful as we possibly can.

It is important to remember, though, that sometimes 'the truth hurts'. The truth can be used as a weapon against another person. Using the truth in this way would be a gross example of insisting on the letter of the precept rather than the spirit. The precepts should always be seen as guidelines for skilful action, not rules or prescriptions to be slavishly obeyed, or to be used hypocritically in order to cause harm. To use the truth in this way would be against the principle of non-injury, which underlies all the precepts; it would be just as unskilful as using untruthfulness to cause harm, or to get our own way.

Mindfulness; and Abstention From Intoxicants

The use (and abuse) of mind-altering drugs is well established in all societies, and the dangers of intoxication and addiction are well known and subject to social controls. From the point of view of the way of action, becoming seriously intoxicated is an abnegation of responsibility for our mental states and actions. If we feel a compulsive need to induce such states, this indicates a lack in other areas of our life. And, to the extent that drug abuse often entails damage to our health, or even a risk of death, it can also indicate lack of self-respect and self-love – qualities that are the basis for the development of kindness and compassion.

Many Buddhists interpret this precept to mean complete abstention from intoxicants, including tea and coffee. Others do not abstain altogether, but maintain strict moderation in the use of intoxicants. The moderate use of alcohol, for example, could mean the occasional glass of beer or wine with a meal, whereas drinking alcohol every day suggests a habit and possible dependence.

The principle of this precept is the maintenance of unimpaired mindfulness or awareness; the bottom line is the avoidance of intoxication. If we find that even a single drink makes us intoxicated or reduces our mindfulness, we need to abstain completely. This would also be appropriate in societies where social drinking is unknown and alcohol is used only to induce drunkenness. Clearly, what applies to alcohol applies to other intoxicants as well.

The Way of Mindfulness

The main reason the precepts include guidance on the use of intoxicants is that intoxication undermines our ability to develop and maintain mindfulness. Mindfulness, or awareness, is a crucial factor at every level of the Buddhist path. Indeed, in one of the Buddha's most important discourses, the *Satipatthana Sutta*, he speaks of the practice of mindfulness as the 'only way' to awakening. What this means is that the path to awakening takes place entirely, and exclusively, within mindfulness. If we are not trying to be mindful, we cannot be said to be on the path to awakening at all.

Thus, in each of the three trainings – the paths of action, meditation, and wisdom – awareness can be seen as the principal feature of the path. In terms of the path of action, this expresses itself as a constant awareness of ourselves and our actions, an awareness that is constantly referring back to the principles of skilful and unskilful action embodied in the precepts.

When we make decisions we are not usually fully aware of our motives. We usually act with the minimum awareness necessary to carry out a task – and sometimes less than that. Training in mindfulness is a very important part of Buddhist practice, and its development is vital to the way of meditation. In terms of ethical action, mindfulness enables us to be as clear as possible about the skilful and unskilful elements in a given situation, to weigh them up in relation to the precepts, and to act accordingly. The more mindful we are, the less likely we are to behave unskilfully. And mindfulness is not something we practise only in certain situations – we can practise mindfulness in all our actions, whether it's washing the dishes, making a phone call, or buying food.

Living with the Precepts

These five precepts, then, direct us towards skilful action in everyday life. Their implications are much more far-reaching than this brief outline can demonstrate, but essentially we have to discover them experientially, by putting them into practice.

The way of skilful action prepares us for our practice of the way of meditation. At the same time, we don't leave it behind it when we embark on the way of meditation. As we will see, the three trainings constantly interrelate: deepening one of them is tantamount to deepening the others as well. The deeper we go into the way of meditation, the more skilful and thoroughgoing our practice of the way of skilful action becomes. The ultimate perfection of the way of wisdom finds expression in the perfection of the ways of action and meditation.

4

THE WAY OF MEDITATION

ONCE A LITTLE-KNOWN PRACTICE associated with Christian monastics, meditation burst on to the modern Western imagination in the 1960s, around the time that the Beatles and other popular figures became devotees of the Maharishi Mahesh Yogi and his Transcendental Meditation. Several decades on, meditation seems to have established a small but enduring niche for itself in Western mainstream culture. Most bookshops carry books on meditation, while glossy healthy-living manuals invariably have a section on meditation as a relaxation technique. People seeking an oasis of calm in their frenetic lives will probably find meditation courses on offer locally. They may even be advised to take it up by their doctor.

The Buddha, of course, did not invent meditation. As we have seen, he practised and perfected several established forms of meditation before eventually discovering a new approach – a way which, unlike the others, enabled him to explore fully the nature of mind and to realize the highest potential of human consciousness. Buddhist meditation, therefore, is about much more than feeling calm and relaxed – although these are valuable aspects of meditative experience. Like Buddhism in general, Buddhist meditation works on the basis that we have unlimited potential to transform our own minds.

WHAT DOES BUDDHIST MEDITATION DO?

In meditation we are concerned mainly with working on our mental states in order to eradicate unskilful states and develop an increasingly continuous stream of skilful ones. Skilful mental states are as central to the way of meditation as they are to the way of skilful action. The main difference is that, as we saw in the last chapter, whilst the way of skilful action involves the development of skilful mental states in relation to external events, the way of meditation involves developing them in our inner experience.

Although the way of skilful action precedes the way of meditation, we don't have to perfect our skilful action before we start to meditate. Many people, in fact, take up meditation first. This is not necessarily counterproductive – it depends how skilful our lifestyle is when we take up meditation. Trying to meditate is a waste of time if we are also doing things that give rise to highly unskilful mental states: for instance, a thief is indulging in unskilful mental states – greed, fear, callousness – that would make meditation very difficult. However, if our lifestyle is already reasonably skilful, an effective meditation practice can be started straight away – and this holds true for people whose lifestyles had previously been deeply unskilful, as attested by prisoners who have taken up meditation while serving their sentence.

After a few weeks, we may well find that some aspects of our lifestyle are hampering our meditation. We then have to make a choice between changing our lifestyle and accepting that our meditation will only go so far. Many meditators who want to act more skilfully begin by practising the five precepts.

TAKING UP MEDITATION

Most people who are new to meditation find it very enjoyable, and see clearly that they are making headway with the practices within a relatively short time. Some even experience profound meditative states very soon after taking up meditation. However, there is another possibility that it is important to be aware of. Occasionally, new meditators can be a little perplexed to find, for example, that they seem to become angry or irritable more readily than before. When this sort of thing happens some, not surprisingly, decide that meditation is not for them.

Such disillusion can be avoided if we approach meditation with a realistic idea of what it does and how it works. Meditation does indeed lead to highly positive, pleasant, and relaxing states – and very much more. From the moment we take it up, we tend to become more aware. This heightened awareness can enable us to enter meditative states; it also means becoming more fully aware of of our *present* mental and emotional states, whatever they happen to be. If there is some suppressed anger, for example, then our meditation simply makes us more aware of it. This is why it can appear to make matters worse. But it is not the meditation that is making us angrier – the meditation makes us more aware of what is there already. Then, crucially, it enables us to change it.

It is impossible to predict precisely what will happen when someone takes up meditation. A few people take to it like ducks to water, most find a good deal of pleasure and interest in the process of self-discovery, and some find it difficult. Everyone who meditates for a number of years experiences each of these responses from time to time – sometimes all within a single session!

The variety and unpredictability of responses to meditation highlight a principle which, as we've already seen, applies to the Buddhist path in general. Buddhist systems of meditation give us a general outline of the likely experiences and stages of progress, but each individual is unique and brings their own personality and conditioning to meditation, so that the experience is never exactly the same for any two people. This is why it is important to learn from an experienced teacher; it is easy enough to learn a meditation technique from a book or audio tape, but these cannot answer our questions or make constructive comments in accordance with our individual needs and qualities.

Personal assistance is especially important when difficulties – or what seem to be difficulties – arise. Although unpleasant and unskilful states can arise in meditation, this does not in itself mean that anything is wrong. We may, for example, have enjoyed some deeply absorbed sessions of meditation and subsequently find ourselves getting unpleasantly irritable whenever we try to meditate. While it would be easy to take this as some sort of failure on our part, the real art of meditation lies in knowing how to deal skilfully with our mental and emotional states, *whatever* they may be.

Our minds are capable of reaching sublime heights, but also of plummeting to profound depths. We can have moments of inspiration, clarity, even bliss, but we can also get caught up in obsessions, hatreds, confusions, and desires. Any of these aspects of ourselves might be uppermost when we come to meditate, depending on our overall physical, mental, and emotional conditions. Naturally, some of these states, as they arise in meditation, are more subjectively pleasant than others, but all of them are aspects of who we are, and all of them can – in fact, must – be brought into the process of self-transformation that meditation entails.

The Two Main Types of Buddhist Meditation

Buddhist meditation practices fall into two principal types. In the first, called 'tranquillity meditation' or more literally 'cultivation of tranquillity' (in Pali, *samatha bhavana*), we are essentially concerned with the cultivation of skilful mental states. We can cultivate them to the point at which we are creating skilful mental states continuously, at least while meditating. In other words, tranquillity – *samatha* – is a continuous but *temporary* stream of skilful mental states.

In the second, 'insight meditation' or 'cultivation of insight' (in Pali, *vipassana bhavana*), we are concerned with overcoming the tendency for unskilful states to reassert themselves when we stop meditating. Our objective here is to see through and ultimately to overcome our fundamental delusion. By destroying delusion, the root of all unskilful action, we give rise to a continuous and *irreversible* stream of skilful mental states. Fully realized, this would be tantamount to awakening itself.

We have to develop tranquillity to a certain extent before we can effectively cultivate insight, and this means approaching tranquillity meditation and insight meditation as two consecutive stages rather than as two alternative methods. In due course, we can bring the two together in a single, concerted approach, but our first task is to explore the cultivation of tranquillity further.

TRANQUILLITY MEDITATION

Taking a break from our daily routine is perhaps the most usual way in which we try to improve our mental states. Getting away from it all, even just finding time for a walk in the countryside, helps us to let go of the tensions and difficulties of everyday life, and allows the mind to become calmer, brighter, and more lucid. Tranquillity meditation produces similar effects, but often much more intensely. Rather than depending on external activities or circumstances, we can directly activate our mind's potential for calm, clarity, emotional positivity, joy, and bliss.

This suggests that there is much more to tranquillity meditation than simply being in a tranquil state. The original Pali term, *samatha bhavana*, is another one that resists efforts to translate it into a single English phrase. *Bhavana* is straightforward enough, meaning meditation in the sense of the cultivation or development of a particular quality. But *samatha*, though literally 'calm' or 'tranquillity', has further connotations in the context of meditation. One of these is *abiding* in tranquillity or calm, that is, maintaining continuous streams of skilful – and therefore tranquil – mental states. At the same time, it connotes the bringing of all our mental and emotional energies into awareness and the cultivation of strong emotional positivity. *Samatha bhavana*, then, means the cultivation of tranquillity of mind, in the sense of stopping or eliminating all unskilful – and therefore untranquil – mental states. So although 'tranquillity meditation' doesn't do full justice to the meaning of *samatha bhavana*, it is a convenient shorthand.

There are many meditation practices for the cultivation of tranquillity, but most of them fall into one of two main types: those for the cultivation of mindfulness and concentration, and those for the cultivation of emotional positivity. These areas overlap and interrelate considerably, but from a practical point of view it helps to approach them separately. Later in this chapter we will look at two widely-used practices that exemplify each of these types: the mindfulness of breathing and the cultivation of loving-kindness. First, though, it is worth reflecting further on the quality of mindfulness itself.

THE DIMENSIONS OF MINDFULNESS

In the last chapter I emphasized the importance of mindfulness at all stages of the Buddhist path. To be mindful means to have an overall, clear awareness of our mental, emotional, and physical states, as well as of our environment – other people, other forms of life, and inanimate things.

There are two main dimensions of our experience to which we need to apply our mindfulness. First, there is the present moment, consisting of whatever our mind perceives – our surroundings and our own mental states. Second, there is the process of which we are a part, especially our direction and purpose – what we have been doing, what we intend to do, and our motivation for doing it. Mindfulness is not in any sense a standing back from life and experience. To be mindful is to be entirely present in whatever we are feeling, thinking, or doing, whilst also being vividly aware of our whole experience as it unfolds.

The ability to be mindful in everyday life depends in turn upon how much we have developed our concentration of mental and emotional energies. It is important to understand exactly what 'concentration' means in the context of Buddhist meditation. We can approach it via a quality that unfortunately is much more familiar to us: distraction. Distraction is diametrically opposed to both mindfulness and concentration; it is a state of mental and emotional dissipation, and lacks any focus or direction.

For most of us, distraction is our normal state, especially when we are doing routine or boring tasks. Essentially it is one of our wrongheaded attempts at satisfaction. We feel discontent about what we are doing, or where we are, so we try to get away from it by distracting ourselves. We may fantasize or daydream whilst performing chores, with the radio or television on at the same time. Being distracted usually means trying to do several things at once (and if we find ourselves doing several things at once, it's a pretty sure sign that we are distracted). Or it could take the form of hopping through a whole succession of tasks without being bothered to complete any of them.

We also seek distraction deliberately, and not just in obvious ways like flopping in front of the television, playing computer games, or window shopping. If we approach any activity – our work, personal relationships, meditation itself – in a habitual and unmindful way, it will become just a distraction from the things we really need to do or the issues we need to face, or simply from experiencing what and who we are at this moment. So what makes something a distraction is not so much the activity itself but the way we approach it. It is possible (though difficult) to watch television mindfully, and it is possible to meditate – or rather to sit down and think we are meditating – unmindfully.

Sometimes we become so distracted that we lose our self-awareness completely. We suddenly realize that we've no idea what we have been doing for the last ten minutes, or we go to fetch something only to forget what it was we wanted. If someone catches us in this kind of state we might say 'Oh, my mind was somewhere else' – but even when we try, we are quite unable to remember where our mind actually was. This is because we have been so distracted, and our awareness has become so spasmodic, that we have temporarily sunk beneath the reflexive quality of consciousness – that is, 'being aware of being aware'.

Reflexive awareness enables us to remember, and to plan ahead – it is the level of consciousness that is characteristically human (which is not to say that it is entirely lacking in other animals). Like most animals, we can usually manage to do simple everyday things without reflexive awareness – or at least with the absolute minimum. But it is rather alarming when, for example, we realize we have driven home from work in this state, since it means that our instincts and habits alone have been in control of the car. In some people, these instincts include dangerous levels of aggression and competitiveness. The less reflexively aware we are, the less responsibility we feel for our actions.

Even in less potentially dangerous circumstances, distraction and lack of self-awareness are clearly undesirable. The lower our level of self-awareness, the duller and more impoverished our experience of life is likely to be. We can try to spice up our life with yet bigger doses of distraction, but this recipe, by its very nature, only ends up makes matters worse. Alternatively we can take the much more creative approach of increasing our mindfulness.

Increasing our level of mindfulness is something for which we all have the capacity. Just consider the way in which people can spontaneously call up amazing levels of one-pointedness, awareness, and concentration when an emergency demands it. Afterwards, they say things like 'I've no idea how on earth I managed to do that,' but the truth is that the potential for acting and living on a higher level is always present. By developing overall mindfulness in conjunction with practices such as the mindfulness of breathing, the qualities that are born out of higher levels of awareness – and the zest for life that goes with them – can become an ever larger part of our life. Ultimately we can develop them to such a degree that we never lose them under any circumstances. But in order to develop them in the first place, we have to overcome our tendency towards distraction by developing the opposite qualities of mindfulness and concentration.

In ordinary use, 'concentration' suggests a vision of furrowed brows and willing ourselves to accomplish something difficult or unpleasant. While this might be a good way to develop a headache, it is not the kind of concentration we nurture in meditation. Meditative concentration – concentrated awareness – is a natural and unforced bringing together of our otherwise scattered mental and emotional energies. It is like the delightful kind of absorption that spontaneously develops when we are totally engrossed in something we find enjoyable and exhilarating – like a musician fully absorbed in playing a piece of music, or a mountaineer totally involved in a demanding climb.

Such heightened awareness is a natural meditative state – one of concentration and general emotional positivity. This is largely what makes such experiences so refreshing and memorable. But, inevitably, most of the time we cannot be doing things that produce concentration in this way. Much of our life is concerned with the apparently commonplace – activities which are so familiar to us that we no longer feel the need to pay them attention. Familiarity all too easily breeds, if not contempt, then disregard. To counteract this tendency we need a more regular and systematic approach, such as that provided by meditation practices like the mindfulness of breathing. In the long run, this is a much more reliable way to develop concentration and deepen mindfulness.

SETTING UP THE CONDITIONS FOR MEDITATION

Meditating is something we can do anywhere at any time – in theory, at least. But for most of us, our immediate conditions have quite an effect on our tendency to distraction. It's best to find a place that is relatively quiet and where we can be undisturbed – which might mean telling others that we are meditating, unplugging the phone, and taking other reasonable precautions.

Whichever meditation you have decided to do, there are several preliminaries to be taken care of. One very important aspect of preparation is the establishment of a comfortable meditation posture. This can vary from sitting on a cushion in the traditional cross-legged posture to sitting in a comfortable upright chair with your feet on the floor. Your back should be straight, neither slumped nor arching backwards, your chin slightly tucked in, and your hands resting lightly on your knees or folded in your lap.

Posture is important because you need to be comfortable and alert for the entire session. It is difficult to meditate effectively if, after a few minutes, you get an excruciating pain in your knee or back, and although physical pain can have other causes, it may be a warning that you are damaging your body in some way. Trying to avoid these problems by lying on your back tends to undermine alertness and you are likely to fall asleep! Setting up a good meditation posture is another area in which it is very helpful to have a personal teacher.

When your posture is as comfortable as possible, you either close your eyes or, with half-closed eyes, let your gaze rest on a single point in front of you. By reducing the stimulus from your external senses you immediately increase your awareness of the mental and emotional levels of your experience. This is where meditation begins. You then start developing more awareness of your immediate experience – what kinds of sensation are arising in your body, what kinds of thoughts and emotions are arising in your mind. This initial stage gives you the opportunity to gently deepen your general level of awareness or mindfulness. Becoming aware of your present experience like this is a much more balanced foundation for the cultivation of concentrated awareness than an attempt to focus on the object of meditation straight away.

THE MINDFULNESS OF BREATHING

Of the many Buddhist meditations created to help us develop concentration, the mindfulness of breathing is one of the most widely used. According to some traditions, this is the meditation the Buddha was doing on the night of his awakening – which suggests that this practice can take a determined meditator a very long way.

THE STAGES OF THE MINDFULNESS OF BREATHING	
	Set up posture
	Develop awareness of your overall present experience, physical, mental, and emotional
1	Be aware of the whole breathing process – counting after the out-breath
2	Be aware of the whole breathing process – counting before the in-breath
3	Be aware of the whole breathing process without counting
4	Be aware of the sensation of the breath at the point where it enters and leaves the body (through the nose)

The mindfulness of breathing, as its name suggests, uses our breathing process as an object upon or around which to develop concentrated awareness. Other concentration practices employ other objects, including colours, sounds, and visualized images, some of which may especially suit people with particular temperaments. But the breath has traditionally been recommended as the best object of concentration because of the way in which it both reflects and enhances our mental and emotional states, and simply because it is always there.

At the start of a session, take time to check your posture and develop an overall awareness of yourself before turning your attention to the sensations of your breath. At first you are concerned with your breath-sensations as a whole. These include the rising and falling of your diaphragm, movements of your chest and abdomen, and the sensation of the breath passing in and out of your nostrils (breathing through the mouth is not recommended unless you have a bad cold). Don't force or manipulate the breath; just be aware of it, however it happens to be, from moment to moment.

There are a number of ways of doing the mindfulness of breathing practice, usually involving several different stages that help the meditator progress towards ever deeper concentration. Most versions of the practice give the meditator extra help in remaining aware of the breathing in the early stages, when concentration is weakest and distraction most likely.

One of these methods, divided into four stages of up to ten minutes each, begins with the use of counting the breaths. The moment the out-breath is completed, you think 'one', after the next out-breath, 'two', and so on until you reach 'ten'. Then you start again at 'one'. Counting helps keep your mind on the breathing by giving your thinking faculty something to hook on to which is directly related to the meditation, rather than leaving it to wander off into unrelated thoughts. So meditation does not involve forcibly stopping our thoughts, but using our thinking faculty – which is naturally present at this stage of the meditation – as a support for the deepening of concentration and awareness.

The breath acts as a kind of centre of gravity, towards which you are gradually reoriented as your breathing attracts more and more of your awareness. At first it might seem very difficult to keep your mind on the breathing, or even to remember that you are supposed to be trying to count the breaths. After a few moments' awareness of the breath, you might find that your mind has somehow floated off, distracted by a thought or daydream or perhaps a noise – a telephone ringing next door reminding you of a call you need to make, for example.

Some of those who are new to meditation find this sort of distraction discouraging and take it to mean that meditation is not going to work for them. Nothing could be further from the truth; distraction and wandering are exactly what is to be expected. If the mind is not very concentrated, it is perfectly natural for it to wander. This is why we need to meditate. The mindfulness of breathing becomes effective in countering distraction as you recollect your purpose and gently return to the breath and the counting. However many times you become distracted, simply return to the breath and start again at 'one'. In this way, little by little, you will get better at keeping your awareness with the breath and weakening your tendency to distraction.

The second stage is a variant on the first, involving a subtle shift of emphasis. Rather than counting *after* the out-breath, you count *before* the in-breath. So just before the in-breath starts, you count 'one', and so on up to ten, as in the first stage. One reason for changing the emphasis, and for having these different stages, is that it helps to keep us on our toes. Otherwise, it is all too easy to lose awareness and carry on counting mechanically. It is even possible to pursue a line of distracted fantasizing in the background, imagining all the time that you are really engaged in the mindfulness of breathing.

The third stage dispenses with the counting. You simply try to remain aware of the overall sensations of the breathing as they happen. Ideally, by this point in the practice, distracting thoughts are arising less and less, so the assistance of counting is no longer necessary. You are in a state of unforced, natural concentration. The fourth and final stage lets you take this even further, by reducing the area of focus from the sensations of the breathing process as a whole to just the sensations created by the breath as it passes in and out through the nose. This allows a much deeper and more subtle, one-pointed concentration to emerge.

However, concentration cannot be guaranteed in any given meditation session; dealing with distractions is often the main concern. Usually, distractions are caused by one of several common hindrances to concentration. Thus, if at some point during the meditation you become aware that you are feeling sleepy or anxious, distracted by sensual fantasies, irritated, or plagued by doubt, then there are various appropriate means that you can use to progress from these states towards steady concentration. These should be learned from an experienced teacher. This brief description is sufficient to give you a taste of the practice, but will not enable you to take it up very effectively.

To meditate effectively is to be aware of our current mental state and to act appropriately to increase awareness and concentration. We need to respond to our meditation experiences in a balanced way. Being too forceful, or wilful, will only lead to the headache-inducing kind of concentration we are trying to avoid. Being too relaxed will lead us into some kind of stupor. Meditative states are a balance between vigour and relaxation, depth and breadth, concentration and awareness, and we have to learn to cultivate and balance these qualities.

How long we will need to practise before we develop meditative states varies greatly from person to person. Many people are fortunate enough to have the combination of enthusiasm and lack of preconceptions known as 'beginner's mind' and experience these states quite soon. Others find that it takes much longer. However, the most important thing to remember is that meditation is a process of self-transformation. Whether or not we experience meditative states is secondary to whether we are dealing effectively with whatever arises in our meditation, be it a distraction, hindrance, or concentrated state.

MEDITATIVE STATES

Sooner or later we will start to notice that the mindfulness of breathing practice is having some effect on us, mainly through our feeling more self-aware. At the very least we will be more aware of the types of distraction and hindrance that tend to plague us, and of the ways in which we can deal with them most effectively. Of course, these distractions and hindrances occur not only in meditation. If we become aware of them arising in meditation, the chances are that they crop up quite a lot in our daily lives, when we tend to be less aware of them. Becoming aware of them in meditation is a step towards being mindful of them – and knowing how to deal with them – in our everyday behaviour. This is one example of the way of meditation feeding back into the way of action.

We are also likely to start to experience states of meditative absorption. At first, our breath may have seemed a rather boring thing to have to observe. But when we become absorbed, it will seem fascinating – more fascinating, in that moment, than anything else we could imagine – and the whole experience becomes richly satisfying. What has changed is not, of course, the breath itself, but the quality of our awareness. When the world appears lifeless and boring to us, it is generally because our mind is dissipated and distracted. In developing meditative states we get rid of distraction and unify our mental energies. This process naturally produces a sense of a much fuller, more intimate engagement with our experience than usual. No external stimulus is needed to produce this intensely alive state – the meditative mind itself learns how to tune into its own energy, brightness, and clarity.

How does meditation affect our awareness? One way of understanding this is to think of meditative states as channels for the integration of our dissipated energies. The current of a river that divides into lots of small rivulets as it passes through a swamp will be weak and the water rather stagnant, but if all the streams re-unite into one course, the current will be powerful and the water fresh. Similarly, if our mental energy is dissipated and distracted, our experience will be at a very low level, but if we bring our mental energies together – integrate them – by directing them at a single object, our experience of our mind, and of the object of meditation, will be greatly enhanced.

States of absorption are characterized by unwavering concentration on the object of meditation combined with lucid awareness and intense pleasure. Once you reach the level of absorption, you can deepen it almost indefinitely. Usually, if you are able to remain concentrated, it will tend to deepen of its own accord, although there are methods to help deepen it. Tradition recognizes between four and nine levels of absorption, which together represent a continuum of ever-deepening and broadening meditative experience.

Whilst we remain in absorption the unskilful states of craving and aversion, and their derivatives, do not arise. Concentration on its own, however, does not necessarily produce skilful mental states. A familiar image from Japanese culture is that of the highly concentrated Samurai swordsman: the sharpness of his concentration in combat means the difference between life and death. This is an excellent and commonly used image for meditation, suggesting both the intensity of concentration required and its vital importance in the

Buddhist life. However, the fact that concentration can be used for killing shows that it is itself a double-edged sword.

In everyday life we often need to concentrate, whether we are tying a shoelace or reading a book. We can concentrate on a skilful activity, an ethically neutral activity, or an unskilful activity. Concentration simply means giving something our undivided attention, but the nature of the object and the nature of our intentions with regard to it make all the difference. Imagine, for instance, the different qualities of feeling when we concentrate on cooking an elaborate meal for some friends, or concentrating on a game of cards in which we've staked too much money. Ethically, the breath is a neutral object. Concentration on the breath will lead to absorption only if we stay in touch with our intention to use this process to eliminate distractions and hindrances.

Absorption can be described as an altered state of consciousness because it is quite different from our normal distracted states. However, there are many ways in which consciousness can be altered and it would be quite misleading to lump them together. Absorption is not, for example, the same as drug-induced states or the kind of trance states in which people lose awareness of themselves and their actions. In absorption we are fully aware and in command of our mind – indeed, much more fully in command of our mind than when we are distracted. People experiencing absorption for the first time often report that 'it seemed very normal' – it somehow feels (if this is not too much of a contradiction) more normal than our normal – distracted – states. We simply feel clearer, brighter, more contented, and completely ourselves.

In the initial levels of absorption, directed thinking is possible – a fact that is crucial for insight meditation. The deeper levels of absorption involve ever-increasing integration and unification of the mind within itself. As our absorption deepens, we naturally reach a point at which our perceptions of the external world cease. Consciousness itself, in an ever-increasingly refined and brilliant state, becomes the entire content of our experience.

For most people, accessing the deeper levels of absorption requires a period of intensive and undistracted meditation. Buddhists who have ordinary lives and jobs make a point of undertaking meditation retreats as often as practicable. If you meditate regularly, you'll find that a week or two of retreat definitely boosts your meditation practice, and provides an opportunity for you to cultivate at least the initial levels of absorption.

DEVELOPING EMOTIONAL POSITIVITY

All tranquillity meditations help us develop greater concentration and integration of our mental energies and, with sufficient practice, to experience continuous streams of skilful mental states. As we have just seen, the mindfulness of breathing is particularly helpful for developing awareness and unifying our mental energies. Another traditional practice, known in Pali as the *metta bhavana*, is primarily concerned with our emotions. It is the most important of a group of four practices which work on this approach to self-transformation.

As we have seen, *bhavana* means meditation in the sense of 'cultivation' or 'development'. *Metta* is much more difficult to translate. It is best understood experientially, by practising the meditation and cultivating metta itself. First, though, it is helpful to see how it relates to our other emotions.

The Quality of Metta

Metta is the opposite of anger and hatred. As such, 'love' would seem to be the natural translation. As we have already indicated, though, this word is open to misunderstanding. By contrast, traditional Buddhist texts use three quite distinct terms to distinguish the meanings encompassed by the English catch-all, 'love'.

Firstly, there is sexual love – often referred to as 'falling in love with' or 'being in love with' someone. It means that we are sexually infatuated with that person, and so compulsively attracted to them, even obsessed by them, that our other human relationships pale into insignificance. 'Love moves mountains,' the saying goes – and it is true that, when in the grip of this emotion, we will do almost anything to ensure its continuation and fulfilment. From a Buddhist point of view, falling in love is primarily an expression of craving – it is love in the most narrow and limited sense.

Secondly, there is what we could call ordinary human love, or warm affection. This is a very important quality: the fond, caring love and affection we feel towards those who are very close and dear to us, whether a friend, relative, sexual partner or, indeed, pet animal. This kind of love can develop within sexual relationships, especially in the longer term, and may either replace or coexist with sexual attraction, but it is not in itself a sexual emotion and we often love people for whom we feel little or no specifically sexual attraction. Warm affectionate love is much less exclusive than sexual love, but it is still selective and limited by the extent of our personal relationships – which effectively excludes the vast majority of living beings.

Thirdly, there is love in its highest sense, which is metta. Metta shares many of the qualities of warm affectionate love. Essentially, it combines strong, active friendliness, kindness, and overt goodwill. But unlike either sexual love or warm affectionate love, metta is totally non-exclusive and without limits. It is neither partial nor possessive, responding equally towards everybody – not only our own species but all living beings.

Metta does not look for anything in return, either overtly or covertly. This distinguishes it very sharply from sexual love, and also, to a degree, from warm affectionate love, which relies fairly heavily on reciprocation. In metta there is no thought of 'what's in this for me?' – our feelings of loving-kindness are as strong towards others as towards ourselves. In its fullest sense, metta is an expression of our limitless capacity for positive emotion – an inexhaustible wellspring which, when allowed to flow unhindered, observes no boundaries or barriers. 'Loving-kindness', then, is perhaps a better translation than 'love', but neither term really does justice to the full power and richness of metta.

Metta is not something that we experience only in meditation. In terms of the Buddhist path, metta is the most basic and important principle of ethical behaviour and relationships – hence its pre-eminence as the positive formulation of the first precept of non-harm. Metta in action takes the form of unfailing friendliness and kindness, and the desire to foster the well-being of others in whatever ways we can. This does not mean, though, that metta demands self-sacrifice in the sense of denying our own welfare, or making ourselves into martyrs: we express metta towards ourselves just as much as towards others.

Metta, then, is a very important quality in the context of the Buddhist path. Clearly, it isn't something we can develop in just a few sessions of meditation – indeed, you may be wondering whether anyone but a saint could develop it at all. However, metta is essentially an intensification and universalization of the warm affection that human beings are naturally capable of feeling and expressing.

This quality provides the basis on which the metta bhavana practice builds.

Many people find this practice very approachable because it deals with the emotions. Others find it more difficult than the mindfulness of breathing, at least initially. This may be because, although we are all capable of human love and affection, we are not necessarily in touch with these emotions when we sit down to meditate. We may be feeling jangled, irritated, depressed, excited, stirred up, emotionally numb, or any of the dozens of emotional states that we go through. So the development of metta is quite a different proposition from the mindfulness of breathing, in which the object of concentration – the breath – is present all the time.

THE CULTIVATION OF LOVING-KINDNESS

Like the mindfulness of breathing, this practice is divided into a number of stages. The first stage is the cultivation of metta towards ourselves. This is the essential basis for the cultivation of metta towards others. However, it is important to start by becoming aware of ourselves as we are now and in particular of whatever emotions we are currently experiencing. We won't be able to cultivate loving-kindness if we begin by denying our current emotional state. Cultivating metta towards ourselves means cultivating it towards the whole of ourselves as we are now, including the negative or unskilful parts. They are an aspect of our present, unawakened, personality – but this does not mean that they are a fixed and unchangeable part of ourselves. Acknowledgment of our emotions is the first step towards transforming them.

Even if we are in quite a strongly negative emotional state such as anger when we sit down to meditate, we can still make some progress towards metta. We might, for example, wish our angry self – which is only a small part of what we are – to be happy and well. This, in itself, can help us to begin shifting the anger – we have generated a little spark of positive intention, encouraging a different emotional quality to emerge that does not identify with the anger. Then it's a question of allowing the non-angry thoughts and emotions to increase, nurturing that little spark of positive intention into a glowing ember until it becomes the effulgent glow of metta.

This is not necessarily easy, because we often get some sort of perverse satisfaction from negative emotions. Even a grey, numb, emotionless state can have an unconscious appeal for us because it insulates us from emotions that we are afraid will be painful or unpleasant. So we often have to make a definite decision to let go of the negativity and consciously cultivate metta. In fact, metta and negative emotions cannot exist simultaneously – metta is a wholly skilful state which, by its nature, precludes unskilful, negative states.

THE STAGES OF THE METTA BHAVANA	
	Set up posture
	Develop awareness of your overall present experience, physical, mental, and emotional
	Become aware of any positive, kindly feelings that you may already have
1	Cultivate metta towards yourself
2	Cultivate metta towards a good friend
3	Cultivate metta towards a 'neutral' person
4	Cultivate metta towards an 'enemy' (a difficult person)
5	Cultivate metta equally towards all four, extending metta without discrimination to all living beings

On the other hand, metta can exist simultaneously with pain. This may seem strange, but it is a significant point. Like any genuinely positive emotion, metta can be cultivated and expressed irrespective of whether we are experiencing pleasure or pain. For example, we may have a headache or a cold but we can still be friendly. We may be experiencing some kind of emotional pain but this does not in itself prevent us from expressing kindness. Metta embodies a skilful and constructive response to whatever circumstances we encounter, especially the more difficult ones.

One of the things that meditation helps us to learn about ourselves is that thoughts and emotions are very fluid and malleable – even those which, for a while, seem to be fixed. We can see this happening outside meditation: for example, our mood can change rapidly from one of vague misery to happiness, simply because someone is genuinely kind to us. But our emotional states do not just happen to us; we are responsible for cultivating them, though very often semiconsciously. So we find that, in meditation, even strong negative emotions can vanish and give way to metta if we are able to make a firm decision not to hang on to them and allow ourselves instead to cultivate a heartfelt wish for our own and others' happiness and well-being. This volitional nature of emotion is what makes it possible for us to change our emotional state and develop metta at all, but this can only start to happen if we want to change.

When we sit down to practise the metta bhavana, we start by becoming aware of how we are right now, in our body, thoughts, and emotions. Then we turn our attention particularly to any positive, kindly feelings that we may already have, whether towards ourselves or someone else. If we can't seem to get in touch with any kindly or friendly emotion, or it seems very weak, we can start to cultivate it. There are various ways of doing this. One traditional approach is to wish ourselves happiness and well-being by silently repeating to ourselves a phrase such as 'may I be happy, may I be well.' It is important to repeat it slowly and with feeling, not mechanically; the effect is a bit like dropping a pebble into a still, clear pool and watching the ripples spread out as the stone sinks – as the ripples die away, we drop in another pebble. Similarly, we express a warm wish towards ourselves and then sit in awareness, allowing its effects to permeate our mind before renewing the wish.

An alternative is to recollect occasions on which we have been emotionally positive, alert, and in tune with life, and to evoke the wish to embody those qualities now. We can also use our imagination to cultivate metta: for example, some people find it helpful to imagine light radiating from their heart, or pouring down upon their head. It is important, though, not to confuse metta with merely pleasant, or nice, feelings. As we have seen, metta is not a feeling of pleasure (or of pain) but a positive emotion – a deliberate expression of well-wishing, friendliness, and kindness.

Approaches such as these may or may not lead directly to the arising of metta in that particular meditation session. But they will certainly, over a period of time, help us develop a greater emotional positivity and open-heartedness which can then be directed into feelings of love and goodwill towards both ourselves and others. This only has to be intensified and universalized in order for it to become metta.

Cultivating metta for ourself is the first of the five stages into which the metta bhavana is divided according to one classic method. In the following three stages, we cultivate metta (or deepen it, if we have already evoked it in the first stage) towards three other individuals.

For the second stage, we choose a friend, someone towards whom we naturally respond with goodwill, kindness, and warmth. We can use the same methods to cultivate metta as those already described, such as directing heartfelt good wishes towards our friend, or recollecting and reliving our emotions when we last experienced a spontaneous upwelling of warm, friendly affection towards them.

In the third stage, we use a similar approach with a person whom we perhaps know by sight but whom we neither like nor dislike – a person who is neutral as far as our emotions are concerned. This can be more difficult as, by definition, we have no particular emotional response to them. On the other hand, it is very easy to tell at this stage whether we have yet managed to develop any genuine metta; if the feeling of warmth we had towards our friend suddenly disappears when we turn our mind to the neutral person, it means the emotion is still coming from partiality towards our friend. If goodwill and friendliness continues unabated, it means that we are beginning to develop real metta.

The fourth stage brings us – imaginatively – face to face with an enemy: that is, someone who usually arouses feelings of dislike and antagonism in us. If we do not have any enemies, we can bring to mind someone towards whom we have less than positive feelings. This could be a colleague or somebody to whom we are emotionally close: a relative, a friend, our children, or our spouse – anyone who has upset us, however much or little and for whatever reason.

In this stage it is very important to put aside the source of the conflict and concentrate simply on wishing that person well. It is also helpful (although not necessarily easy) to recall things that we do appreciate about that person. This helps us to get a sense of perspective that in turn undermines our negative – unskilful – feelings towards that person. Such negative emotions can take a long time to break down, but by taking responsibility for them and meeting them head on in this way they can usually be resolved in the end.

The friend, neutral person, and enemy embody for us the three main emotional responses that we have towards other living beings: attraction, indifference, and aversion. The underlying principle of this practice is that if, for example, we can feel metta towards one neutral person, then we are not very far from feeling it towards all neutral people; likewise with friends and people whom we dislike. In the fifth and final stage of the practice we put this into effect. First

we bring together in our mind the people from the earlier stages –
ourselves included – and try to cultivate a completely equal quality
and strength of metta towards them all. Then we extend our metta
without discrimination to all living beings whatever. This is the
culmination of the practice: the stage at which we can realize the
totally impartial, unlimited, universal nature of metta. If we haven't
yet developed any metta, simply directing whatever degree of
warmth and friendliness we have cultivated towards all beings in the
universe is in itself a very effective way of evoking it.

As mentioned earlier, the metta bhavana is the most important of
a group of four related meditation practices concerned with the
cultivation of positive emotion. Metta is the fundamental positive
emotion in Buddhism, but it can take various forms, according to the
situation. If we have developed metta and then come across suffering
of any kind, our metta will by its very nature transmute into compassion – a strong impulse to act in order to alleviate the suffering in
whatever way we can. If, on the other hand, we come across other
people's happiness or good fortune, metta will naturally turn into the
quality of sympathetic joy – a feeling of intense pleasure in others'
happiness (the opposite of envy or jealousy). Both compassion and
sympathetic joy can be cultivated through meditation, in practices
similar to the metta bhavana. So, too, can the fourth – and most
profound – of these positive emotions: equanimity. This is a quality
that synthesizes metta, compassion, and sympathetic joy and yet
transcends them – a quality which has been described as 'vibrant
peacefulness'.

The metta bhavana, the mindfulness of breathing, and all the other
tranquillity meditation practices are indispensable in enabling us to
deepen self-awareness and cultivate vibrantly positive states. But the
cultivation of tranquillity is only one side of the coin. If we are to
make these states irreversible and, like the Buddha, discover for
ourselves the answer to the problem of suffering, we need also to
cultivate insight – and that is the subject of the next chapter.

5

CULTIVATING INSIGHT

AS WE SAW in the last chapter, meditation can give us our strongest experience of concentration, lucid awareness, and positive emotion. To the extent that these are completely skilful states of mind, meditative absorption gives us a glimpse of awakening, but – as the Buddha himself discovered – there are important differences between absorption and the awakened state itself.

After his awakening, the Buddha categorized the meditative states he had experienced under his first two teachers as belonging to the deepest levels of absorption. He had not at that time had any direct experience of what it might be like to be awakened, but he could see that these absorptions were not what he was looking for. He was able to do this because he was completely clear about what he was seeking: a real – that is, permanent – solution to the problems of life and death. When he experienced for himself the meditative absorptions that his teachers regarded as the highest possible spiritual realization, he immediately saw that, though they took him entirely beyond outer sense experience and were very refined and blissful states of consciousness, they were nevertheless temporary states of mind. Whilst he was in deep absorption, the problems did indeed vanish; but when he came out of it – as he had to do eventually, if only to eat and drink – they reappeared.

Such a temporary solution was little better than no solution at all, especially if it could be experienced only whilst sitting motionless and entirely detached from the outer senses. Siddhartha knew that his goal could not be a transitory experience, however blissful and skilful in itself. Awakening had to become the very basis of his being.

His next direction, the path of extreme asceticism, took him no closer to his goal; but at last he found the door to awakening through the recollection of the spontaneous meditative experience of his childhood. This led him to his greatest discovery: the means to develop insight into the true nature of things – the way things really are. This was what set the Buddha's system of teaching apart from anything that had been taught before. Many gurus had taught ways to reach deep absorption; only the Buddha taught the way of insight *combined* with absorption as a means to transform and reconstruct human nature at the very deepest level.

PREPARING THE GROUND

In Buddhist systems of meditation, then, absorption – tranquillity meditation – is practised not as an end in itself but in order to develop the basis for the cultivation of insight. Meditation is a blind alley if it leads to higher absorptions without the cultivation of insight because, as Siddhartha himself discovered, absorption is in itself a very desirable state. The deeper the absorption, the more desirable it is – so much so that someone who can dwell in the formless absorptions at will may not wish to go any further, or even to do anything else at all. In this way, an advanced meditator can become as hooked on absorption as many people are on sex. Such attachment is an expression of craving and delusion – and hatred is never very far away from these – so it is clear that absorption practised for its own sake brings us no nearer to awakening, and can even be a major obstruction.

This danger is reflected in a recurring theme in Indian mythology: a sage sits in a cave for years, deep in blissful absorption, only to fall madly in love with a passing maiden – or become furiously angry – the moment he leaves his cave. A variation on this is found in the story of the great Buddhist adept Saraha. In the early part of his spiritual career, he is said to have sat down to meditate just as his wife was preparing a delicious radish curry for supper. He entered a very deep absorption and remained there completely motionless for twelve years. But this did not prevent him, the moment he opened his eyes, from indignantly asking why his radish curry wasn't ready!

For most of us, though, addiction to the higher absorptions is unlikely to be a problem. Few people, particularly in the West, feel able to commit themselves to the long-term, full-time practice of tranquillity meditation required to develop such states. In any case, the cultivation of insight does not depend on the higher absorptions. As we saw in Chapter 1, Siddhartha discovered the way to a meditative state in which – unlike in the higher absorptions – directed thought was still possible. We need to have cultivated this through our practice of tranquillity meditation before we take up insight meditation.

We need a deeper, concentrated level of awareness in order to cultivate insight simply because if we approach it distractedly or half-heartedly it will have no effect. The cultivation of insight demands that we apply as much of ourselves as possible to the task. Insight meditation involves transforming all levels of our being, not just the parts of which we are conscious in our normal, relatively distracted states. The more of ourselves we can to bring to our meditation, the more effectively we will be able to transform the deeper levels of our being where the roots of craving, aversion, and delusion lie.

In addition, for effective insight practice, we need strong, refined positive emotion. This is because the cultivation of insight involves looking steadily and directly at matters that we may find intensely threatening. In fact, from our ordinary ego-clinging point of view, insight is like death. What has to die, and what feels threatened, is our self-view, formed from delusion and the inseparable attributes of clinging, attachment, and fearful aversion. But even though our self-view *is* just a delusion, to us it seems virtually synonymous with life itself. We literally cannot imagine existing without it.

To attack self-view head on, as we do when we cultivate insight, can give rise to experiences that will shake us to our roots. That is why strong metta is essential. Metta helps not only because it is highly skilful and positive but also because it is a state in which our self-orientation is already greatly reduced. If we are nurturing equal metta towards everybody, ourselves included, we have less inclination to be protective towards what we regard as 'me' and 'mine'.

CREATING THE CONDITIONS FOR INSIGHT

Insight is not a matter of seeing into some separate, other reality. In essence, as we have seen, insight means seeing *into* and seeing *through* our misperceptions regarding the reality that we are a part of, here and now. In this way, through insight, we come to experience things as they really are, unclouded by delusion. Reality is in front of our noses all the time, whether we recognize it or not, and this means that we can use *any* element of our experience as a means of cultivating insight.

Recognizing this, the various forms of Buddhism have developed many different methods of insight cultivation which can help us become ever more attuned and receptive to the way things really are, according to the Buddha's insight. All Buddhist methods of insight cultivation have the same ultimate objective: the arising – or realization – of insight itself.

A well-known story from Zen Buddhism tells of a Buddhist nun, Chiyono, who was carrying a bucket of water. Suddenly, without warning, the bottom of the bucket fell out, and at that very instant she realized insight into the way things really are.[6] By reflecting on this incident we may get a feel for how the *cultivation* and the *arising* of insight relate to each other.

Such small accidents happen to everyone. How do we respond? We might mutter a swearword or two and then start clearing up, irritated by the inconvenience. If we are already feeling a bit annoyed or irritable, we might even get really angry. Either of these responses is, of course, an expression of our basic delusion. All they succeed in doing is confirming, deepening, and prolonging that delusion. Needless to say, this is the very opposite of any kind of insight cultivation.

On the other hand, if we have been cultivating insight for some time, we might momentarily be thrown by the accident but then remember that it offers us an opportunity to cultivate insight. Perhaps it would remind us that things are by nature subject to decay and dissolution, which is why it is foolish to depend on them in an unrealistic way. Such a reflection should help us to let go of the accident and carry on in a more positive and skilful mental state.

This is an example of insight *cultivation*, but it is clearly not what occurred in Chiyono's case. She was not put out by the accident, nor did she need to engage in any reflection on it. Insight simply arose. However, it did not arise out of the blue. By the time of the incident, Chiyono had been cultivating insight through meditation, and in her everyday life in the Zen monastery, for many years. This is why she was so profoundly receptive to the implications of such an everyday kind of accident.

This is not to say, though, that the arising of insight was a direct and inevitable outcome of her insight practice. This is an important point. There is no guarantee that any particular method or technique – even if it is called insight meditation – will itself lead to the arising of insight. The arising of insight is in a sense completely outside our control – we cannot *make* it happen. Insight – at least from our unawakened point of view – is completely extraneous to everything we think of as 'me'. What we think of as our 'self' has absolutely no control over it – indeed, the very tendency to think of insight as an 'it' that we might 'have' or 'own' is to miss the point entirely. To have insight means to see through our ordinary, deluded self-view and, ultimately, to abandon what we normally think of as 'me'.

Though we cannot make insight arise, what we *can* do is cultivate the conditions that make it more likely to arise. It is like constructing a lightning conductor: the conductor does not *make* lightning strike it but, if we put one up, sooner or later it will probably be struck. Similarly, by cultivating insight we gradually imbue ourselves with an awareness and appreciation of the way things really are, according to the Buddha's teaching. This is not the same as knowing it directly through our own experience, but by engaging in insight cultivation we are making ourselves increasingly open and receptive to it. As long as we continue in this way, circumstances will eventually arise that allow us to see directly into and through at least an aspect of our deluded self-view.

PRACTISING INSIGHT REFLECTION

Life is full of opportunities to cultivate insight, and we have to be ready to embrace them whenever they occur. Ideally we would use every single situation, which would mean making the cultivation of insight an integral part of our mindfulness practice, and having a continuous awareness of the insight potential of our experience. However, we need to start with something a lot less demanding, such as a basic insight reflection.

We can practise insight reflection as a formal meditation practice or within other contexts, for example while quietly walking or sitting on our own. As a focus for our reflection, we could take up the topic of impermanence. We might start by reflecting on what impermanence means: that everything we perceive as existing in time must necessarily be changing, even if that change is imperceptible. If we are not convinced of this, we could try to think of something that is truly permanent. Are atoms permanent and unchanging? Is the universe as a whole permanent and unchanging? Does permanence apply to anything between these two (provisional) extremes? Having reflected on impermanence in this more general and abstract way, we could then apply our reflections directly to ourselves and our experience even as we are reflecting: 'My mental and emotional states are changing all the time, my body is changing as I get older.' This could give rise to the thought: 'One day, I am going to die.'

If we are quiet, calm, and concentrated, our reflections will have a far stronger effect on us than when we are distracted. Impermanence will become much more of a reality for us. We may even, for a moment, really know that we are going to die – not as a concept or an idea, but as a fact. This, in a very small way, would be an insight.

We can use any Buddhist teaching on wisdom as a basis for reflection. (The next chapter covers the most important of these.) There are also many structured insight reflections that are more suited to formal meditation than to ad-lib reflection. One of these is known as the 'contemplation of the six elements'.

The Six Elements Meditation

The six elements of earth, water, fire, air, space, and consciousness represent the main constituents of our experience and of the universe itself. In this meditation we contemplate each element in turn, in order to get to grips with the fact that they are not *owned* by us. The nature of things is such that we cannot ultimately possess or cling to anything.

Taking the earth element first, we might start by recollecting things that have the earth-like quality of hardness and resistance – rocks, trees, apples, bricks, tables, books, and so on. Then we would contemplate the parts of our body that have this quality – hair, teeth, bones, and muscles. Having established some feeling for the earth element in this way, we could then reflect that the earth element within our body comes entirely from the earth element outside our body. It comes from the food we eat, which renews our living cells. In turn, waste and dead cells leave the body, by way of excretion, to return to the earth element outside. In the end, when we die, the earth element which seems to be ours will have to be given up altogether, whether we like it or not. So having – to some extent – taken in the fact that the earth element is not and cannot be ours, we reflect that we will only suffer if we try to hang on to it, or define ourselves by it.

We then reflect in a similar way on the other elements that make up our experience of ourselves and the universe, focusing on each of them as objects of our attachment – things that we cling to as 'me' or 'mine'. The water element exists in the world in oceans, rivers, and rain, and within us as blood, saliva, urine, and so forth. The nature of water is to flow – it flows straight into us, and straight out again, and when we die it will finally return to the water element in the universe. So water, also, cannot be grasped.

The 'fire element' in our bodies takes the form of the heat constantly generated by our metabolism. It cannot be grasped because it constantly radiates away from us. The element of air flows in and out of our body all the time. And we are part of the 'space element' – that is, a location in space – only until our death and our body's dissolution.

Finally, consciousness, together with the objects of consciousness, cannot be grasped or held on to. Consciousness consists of our thoughts, emotions, feelings, and other mental functions. To most people, their mind or consciousness seems to be the essence of what they are; but if it is examined and reflected upon, it can be seen to consist of processes alone. There is no one particular fixed thing that is 'my' consciousness. So consciousness is no more the real, permanent self that we believe ourselves to be than are the other elements.

The six elements meditation helps us gradually to penetrate the fact that not only do the elements not belong to 'me', but neither is a 'me' that owns them to be found. In this way, the meditation gradually undermines our 'grasping at a self'.

There are many insight meditation practices of this sort, some simple, some very complex. For example, on the complex side, certain meditations used in Tibetan Buddhism start with what amounts to a rigorous training in logic, which establishes a firm intellectual conviction of the truth of a doctrine, and then proceed with numerous systematic reflections based on this understanding.

INSIGHT PROVOKED BY A TEACHER

A quite different approach, especially characteristic of Zen and tantric Buddhism, depends on the teacher using any means at their disposal to induce in the pupil a direct experience of insight. Some of the best-known examples of these are among the most extreme.

One story concerns an impudent young Zen monk who kept imitating a particular gesture that his Zen master, Gutei, made with his finger when teaching.[7] When Gutei came to hear about this, he went in search of the young man, seized his hand, and without a word cut off the offending finger with a knife. The astonished young monk cried out and started to run away, but Gutei called and stopped him. As the young monk turned his head, the master raised his own finger, and at that very moment the young man realized insight.

Another story illustrating this very direct approach comes from the Indian tantric tradition. It is about the eleventh-century guru Tilopa, who put his disciple Naropa through a lengthy series of extremely painful experiences before he would grant him the tantric teachings. On one occasion the two of them were walking along a road when a prince and his bodyguards came riding towards them in a chariot. Tilopa casually said, 'Any real disciple of mine would drag this prince from his chariot and push him around a bit.' Naropa instantly did just that and, not surprisingly, the bodyguards beat him to within an inch of his life. But as a result he gained a vital insight into the strength of his attachment to his own body.

Stories such as these are easily misunderstood. They represent the ability of a master who has genuinely realized insight to seize on anything in order to help the disciple cut through ego attachment. This always takes place in a context of complete mutual trust and an intensive shared practice of the Dharma. Any mere imitation of such approaches, based on superficial understanding without insight, would be disastrous. In any case, these are unusually extreme examples; the approach is much more usually fostered in a less spectacular but nevertheless effective way, sometimes in a formal or ritual context, and sometimes very informally.

Although particular schools of Buddhism often emphasize either reflection or direct introduction by the teacher, the two approaches are by nature complementary rather than exclusive. Both require a firm foundation in skilful action and the tranquillity meditation in order to succeed. And both approaches need to be followed by a further stage – the stabilization of insight.

STABILIZATION IN INSIGHT MEDITATION

Stabilization is a specifically meditative element of the cultivation of insight. It means having reached a point of full absorption in the subject of the insight meditation, whatever it is. Insight meditation necessarily begins with a relatively superficial awareness of the meditation object; stabilization represents a deeper and more experiential awareness of the object with all the intensity and positivity of a state of absorption. For example, in reflecting on impermanence, the relatively superficial level involves thinking along the lines of 'things are impermanent, my experience now is impermanent,' and so on. As the meditation proceeds, this conceptual activity becomes increasingly subtle. Stabilization is the stage when we simply *know*, directly, that whatever we are aware of from moment to moment is impermanent.

In stabilized insight meditation there is an element of what could be called conceptualization, but this is very different from our ordinary thinking processes. Stabilization involves our most creative and flexible thinking ability working completely in harmony with our most positive emotional energies. This makes our awareness very subtle, powerful, and incisive, and at the same time highly skilful, open, and receptive to the object of insight. Stabilization is still an aspect of insight cultivation rather than an arising or realization of insight; it is, however, the most direct and effective form of insight cultivation.

The more we cultivate this deepest kind of insight meditation, the more the truth about the way things really are will tend to permeate our life and awareness. Whether or not any insights arise, our life will tend to become ever more deeply imbued with this insightful outlook. We will also become increasingly able to use day-to-day situations to help us to cultivate insight.

The more we practise this intense insight cultivation, the more we will experience a kind of tension. On the one hand there will be our delusion or self-view, which – to the extent that insight has not yet arisen – will have as tenacious a hold as ever. On the other hand our strong cultivation of insightful awareness will gradually be making it less and less possible for us to hold on to our deluded self-view. On a basic, existential level, this will be a very uncomfortable state. We are caught between a rock and a hard place, and something will eventually have to give. If there is enough momentum behind our practice of skilful action and meditation, what will 'give' will be our deluded self-view itself – insight having arisen to take its place. To put this another way, from this moment, the tendency at the very core of our being will no longer be delusion, but wisdom.

This marks the transition from the way of meditation to the way of wisdom. Someone who has reached this point is not yet fully awakened because the ramifications of delusion are subtle and extensive. It is rather like having cut through the root of a thorny creeper smothering a tree – even though there is still a good deal of prickly disentangling to do, it is only a matter of time before the creeper withers and falls away.

As even this brief description indicates, the cultivation of insight is a far more demanding and long-term task than the cultivation of absorption. Some degree of absorption can be developed quite rapidly, even by someone who is new to meditation, but there is no short cut to insight. Cultivating and realizing permanent changes to the very core of our being can only be brought about through many years of intensive, patient, and untiring Dharma practice.

6

THE WAY OF WISDOM

WISDOM PERMEATES BUDDHISM so completely that we have already touched on several of its aspects: the four truths, the three levels of understanding, the meaning of insight, and the nature of our deluded self-view. This chapter looks at what is involved in practising the way of wisdom, and the next chapter looks at some of the main teachings on wisdom and how they point to the way things really are.

The development of wisdom is both the destination and the path of Buddhism – both the snow-capped peak and the journey that brings us to it, to use that earlier metaphor. Undertaking the Buddhist path means developing wisdom at ever profounder levels, and manifesting compassion to ever greater degrees. The realization of wisdom at the highest level is awakening itself; but we can cultivate wisdom at all stages of the Buddhist path in one way or another, right from the beginning. This is possible because, as we saw in Chapter 2, the practice of wisdom starts on the level of rational understanding and progressively deepens until, ultimately, it becomes unshakeable realization. Insight and wisdom are not really two different things: if an insight arises, the result is a state of wisdom.

Buddhists do not, of course, have a monopoly on insight. Spontaneous insight can arise for any number of reasons: for example, direct experience of some kind of trauma, such as a serious illness, a major loss, or the death of somebody close; or through the acute awareness of the suffering of others caused by oppression, war, or famine. Whatever the cause, the arising of insight can have a very strong effect on people. Usually it stimulates them to examine and reappraise their lives and their values – and some, sooner or later, decide to follow up their spontaneous glimpse of insight by embarking on a spiritual path such as Buddhism.

The spiritual path provides us with a context in which to understand and develop these spontaneous insights. Otherwise, even a profound and deeply moving experience eventually fades and loses its significance. Old ways of acting and relating to others can eventually re-assert themselves, simply by force of deeply entrenched habit. All genuine insight experiences are by nature ego-threatening (and conversely, most ego-threatening experiences are to some degree of the nature of insight). While some people may grasp the implicit significance of such an experience and be able to assimilate it to some extent, others may fail to understand its meaning, or just find it disturbing and wish to forget it as quickly as possible – a wish that their threatened self-view is only too happy to encourage. Very few people have spontaneous insight experiences that are sufficiently deep and overwhelming to bring about permanent change, but for those who have had such an experience, Buddhism as a whole, and the way of wisdom in particular, provides a way to understand it, deepen it, and realize its implications.

People take up the Buddhist path for other reasons, of course. Most people who become Buddhists (or are born into a culture where Buddhism is prominent) will not have had spontaneous experience of insight. If that is the case, Buddhism enables us to embark on the way of wisdom by helping us to understand what wisdom is, and by providing means for its development.

UNDERSTANDING WISDOM AT THE THREE LEVELS

The word 'wisdom' is the one normally used to translate the Sanskrit *prajna*, which can also be translated as 'really knowing' or 'understanding'. Whatever our motivation for pursuing our interest in Buddhism, our initial explorations will inevitably lead to a rather approximate, rough and ready understanding of the Dharma – in effect, understanding through learning. If we then go on to deepen and clarify this initial understanding by reflecting on it and encouraging it to percolate into every area of our life, we will be developing the second level of understanding. Finally, if by meditating on it ever more deeply and wholeheartedly we transform our lives in accord with that understanding, we have reached the third level of understanding – the level that consists of both stabilized insight meditation and the arising of insight itself. In practice, at any one time we will probably find ourselves dealing with some aspects of the Dharma at the first level and others at the second or third level.

Cultivating the three levels of understanding can also be seen in terms of the development of *right view* – the first step on the noble eightfold path. The Buddhist teachings on wisdom were given by the Buddha and other awakened human beings to convey – in so far as it could be expressed in words – their insight into the way things really are. These teachings give us perspectives with which to examine our own views, and especially our self-view.

What we are concerned with here are not views in the sense of opinions, such as those we might have about politics, sport, or fashion. However passionately we feel about these topics, the views that the teachings encourage us to examine are, as it were, the views *behind* the views. What are the underlying views that can make someone so passionate – even, in extreme cases, violent – about an opinion such as who ought to have won a football match? Such views embody our deepest implicit false assumptions about ourselves and the world in which we live. They are expressions of delusion, manifesting as craving or aversion, and it is this that makes them 'wrong views'.

Under the spell of wrong views, we see things as they are *not*. The eradication of wrong views, and the corresponding development of views which harmonize with the way things really are, is a process which continues along the entire Buddhist path at ever more subtle levels. At the level equivalent to understanding through learning, we develop right view by gaining a clear understanding of what awakened people have taught about the way things really are, and of how this relates to the way we, as unawakened people, see the world.

If we are to develop wisdom fully, we need to start with a clear *conceptual* understanding of the teachings on wisdom. However, this certainly doesn't mean that the Buddhist path is only for scholars and intellectuals. The essential truths of these teachings are not conceptually difficult (though Buddhist scholars have produced plenty of conceptually difficult commentaries on them). Among the Buddha's immediate disciples there were quite ordinary, uneducated people who were able to penetrate to the depths of his teaching very quickly. Some needed to hear little more than a brief outline such as 'all things are impermanent' in order to become awakened. Wherever it has spread, Buddhism has developed forms and expressions that are appropriate for all kinds of people. The difficulties we encounter in understanding the Buddhist teachings on wisdom are not so much conceptual as emotional – even existential. They represent a perspective on our lives which is so at odds with our usual views and assumptions that we strongly resist their implications.

To practise Buddhism effectively, it is not enough to have just a conceptual appreciation of the Buddhist teachings – we need a heartfelt response to them as well. Understanding the truth of unsatisfactoriness in theory is very different to seeing how our choices in life can lead directly to suffering for ourselves and others. Only a strong rational *and* emotional response to Buddhist teaching will be enough to motivate us to persevere with the tremendous project of transforming all aspects of our life.

DEVELOPING WISDOM

As we have seen, we begin to follow the way of wisdom in the full sense when our practice of the ways of action and meditation bear fruit in a profound insight – an irrevocable seeing-through of our deluded self-view. As a result of this, delusion ceases to be the effective core of our being. This is perhaps the most important point in the entire Buddhist path, arguably even more momentous than awakening itself. It is often referred to as 'irreversibility' because, once we have passed it, it is simply impossible for us to return to our deluded state. Having seen beyond doubt that self-view is a delusion, we cannot remain unawakened. It is as if a greater amount of our total being is now oriented towards awakening than towards delusion.

A traditional metaphor for this level of insight is 'stream entry'. Just as a boat that has entered the current of a great river will inevitably be carried to the sea, so someone who has seen right through their delusion has entered the 'stream' of insight that will inevitably lead to awakening. Tradition holds that a 'stream entrant' will gain full awakening within at most seven lifetimes. According to the Pali canon, some stream entrants have realized full awakening within weeks – and the Buddha himself realized all the stages between stream entry and full awakening in the course of a single night.

Irreversible insight – stream entry – marks the stage at which someone fully enters the way of wisdom; but such insight can arise only when they have intensively practised all three trainings: not only the ways of action and meditation but the way of wisdom as well. As we have seen, it is possible to practise wisdom through learning and reflecting before fully entering the way of wisdom through direct experience.

The relationship between the three trainings is one of continuous, creative interaction. For instance, we might find that overcoming an unskilful habit leads to a general strengthening of our mindfulness and meditation. This in turn enables us to study the teachings on wisdom more penetratingly and to cultivate insight more effectively. As a result, we might gain an important insight into the nature of our deluded self-view and deepen our understanding of how this influences our behaviour towards others. Such an insight would undoubtedly affect the way in which we behave in future – which brings us back to the path of skilful action.

The dynamic is, of course, much more complex than this, as we need to be practising aspects of each of the three trainings simultaneously, and each is continually affecting the others. But the overall consequence is that, over the years, our practice of each of the trainings will become ever more effective and ever more imbued with the qualities of insight and wisdom.

FROM INITIAL TO IRREVERSIBLE INSIGHT

The insights that arise before stream entry (which we will call initial insights) and those that arise afterwards are not two different types of insight; the main difference is that the first kind is reversible and the second is not. Initial insights weaken our delusion, but they are not sufficiently strong in themselves to undermine it completely. Initial insights are extremely important, however, because it is through their cumulative effect that the irreversible insight of stream entry arises.

As we saw at the beginning of this chapter, traumatic experiences such as illness, loss, or death can precipitate insight in anybody, whether or not they have heard of Buddhism. But we continually have many other opportunities to develop insight, and Buddhists aim to make the most of these. The more progress we have made with the three trainings, the more effectively we will be able to use the opportunities for insight that present themselves. Any experience that brings us face to face with our delusion is one in which we can develop wisdom. Since delusion is the basis for most of our responses to life, such opportunities can present themselves many times every day.

For instance, we might be looking forward to a treat that doesn't subsequently materialize, or that doesn't turn out as we had hoped. Our normal response will probably be to feel put out or upset. We might feel like blaming other people, the weather, or whatever it is that has prevented us from getting what we want. However, if we were trying to cultivate wisdom, we could instead reflect on how delusion underlies such reactions. We would recognize our disappointment, but at the same time try to see that this is the result of our craving for life to run according to plan. We could reflect that this craving has made us suffer the pain of disappointment because it is not in accord with the way things really are: we cannot expect things to happen just because we want them to happen.

Even apparently trivial events are potential doorways to wisdom. A leaf blowing about in the wind could remind us of the truth that all things are impermanent, or at least we could use this as an opportunity to reflect on impermanence. The story of Chiyono in the previous chapter is an example of the potential impact of everyday experiences.

Until we experience irreversible insight, it is as if we are separated from reality (the way things really are) by a thick, opaque veil that makes reality invisible to us; but the more we foster insight, the thinner and more transparent the veil becomes. This image shouldn't be taken too literally: there is nothing that actually separates our perceptions from reality. What we perceive *is* reality, but our delusion distorts it and leads us to misinterpret it. Bearing this in mind, we can think of initial insights as moments when the veil becomes transparent enough for us to discern what lies on the other side – and the stronger the insight, the more transparent the veil, and the more clearly we see. At the same time, although what we see is reality, our perception of it is limited by the uneven transparency of the veil.

The veil represents the sense of separation (or duality) that we maintain between what we experience as 'self', or subject, and what we experience as 'other', or object. An initial insight is one in which we provisionally or temporarily see through our assumption that there are two entirely separate kinds of thing in the universe – that is, things that are part of our ego-identity, and things that are not. This dualistic assumption is not in accord with the way things really are – as the meditation on the six elements helps us to see. What we perceive as self and as other are in fact constantly flowing into and out of each other.

With insight, we see with unusual clarity exactly how the dualistic mind makes us crave some things, wanting them as part of ourselves, and feel aversion towards others, wanting nothing to do with them. We briefly glimpse the absurdity of this way of living – how we cause suffering both to ourselves and to others by being so attached to this, or so fearful about that. We can at least glimpse how these ways of relating to the world are delusions of our own making and have nothing to do with reality.

So any experience of insight will weaken our dualistic belief in a separate self and other, which is integral to our deluded self-view. However, initial insights do not see into our subtler dualistic assumptions. In particular, we still experience ourselves – our self or ego – as separate from the object of insight. To put it another way, although there is genuine penetration into the way things really are, our deluded ego subtly appropriates it: we might think, 'I am having this insight,' and with this would come a very subtle pride or grasping at it. This kind of response is unavoidable in the case of initial insights, which is why they offer only a limited experience of reality. Initial insights are not yet a direct knowledge of reality as the very nature of our being and experience; this is what distinguishes them from irreversible insight. With initial insights, we see *into* our delusion, but not yet *through* it at the very deepest level.

In terms of our image of the veil, it is as if initial insights have the effect of weakening the fabric, making it thinner and more fragile, so that, sooner or later, a hole appears in the veil. The barrier between our perceptions and reality has now been breached. This represents the moment at which irreversible insight arises. For the first time, the duality between ego (or, rather, what we have always taken to be our ego) and insight – the way things really are – is altogether transcended. The insight that causes this to happen is not different in kind from the initial insights that have preceded it. It is more as if the cumulative effect of initial insights has worn away all but the flimsiest of threads – one more insight, even one more tiny increment of insight, and it's all too much for our poor old self-view.

As with any kind of delusion, our recognition means that we are no longer taken in by it. From the moment that insight becomes irreversible, delusion ceases to be the effective core of our being. Like a mirage, it disappears – to be replaced for good by its exact opposite, wisdom. To put this another way – which, given the limitations of language, is just as true – piercing the veil of delusion reveals the wisdom that was always there. Whichever way we think of it, the core of our deluded self-view, together with its dualistic view of things, is seen through beyond any possibility of our taking it seriously or literally again. This complete certainty about the delusory nature of the self or ego is what makes awakening inevitable.

FROM IRREVERSIBLE INSIGHT TO AWAKENING: BREAKING THE FETTERS

Although our irreversible insight would mean that we were now in effect more awakened than unawakened, we'd only be at the beginning of the way of wisdom in the full sense. There is still a way to go before we are fully awakened. In terms of the image of the veil, although there is now a hole in it, and the veil is very thin and transparent, it is not yet altogether gone. In other words, while irreversible insight means having seen through the core of our delusion, there are still subtler manifestations of it which need to be eradicated.

A traditional way of looking at these more subtle manifestations of delusion is in terms of the ten 'fetters' that hold us back from full awakening. These fetters embody all aspects of delusion, starting with the grossest and finishing with the most subtle. We enter the way of wisdom in the full sense when the arising of irreversible insight breaks the first three fetters that together make up the core of our delusion. The first of these is self-view itself – the conviction that we are or have a separate, unchanging self which can get what it wants and reject what it does not want. When we fully see through this, we also see through the second and third fetters – two mental-cum-emotional habits that are intimately bound up with this self-view.

The second fetter, sceptical doubt, is a kind of determined mental and emotional fuzziness, a vested interest in not seeing things clearly. We frequently express this kind of thing in rationalizations, such as 'Well, it won't do any harm if I have just the one cigarette.' Sometimes this is quite unconscious, but usually we are more than half aware of our own self-deception. This partial awareness makes it all the more important – if we are going to get what we want – to convince ourselves that it is fine to go ahead by remaining obstinately unclear about the issues. This kind of doubt is not the honest, questioning doubt that seeks the truth, however unsettling – on the contrary, it seeks to avoid facing up to reality. In relation to Buddhist teaching and practice, this woolly self-interested rationalization often appears as scepticism: 'Well, maybe that's *not* the way things really are,' or 'Who is the Buddha to say that this or that is unskilful?' The subtext in either case is that we are determined to do what we want to do – and if this happens not to be in accord with the way things really are, well, so much the worse for the way things really are. In reality, of course, it is so much the worse for us.

THE TEN FETTERS			
1	**Self-view**	The conviction that we are, or have, a separate, unchanging self	
2	**Sceptical doubt**	Self-interested rationalization which takes the form of scepticism	Broken together = stream entry
3	**Dependence on moral rules and religious observances**	The tendency to define things and take the definition literally, approaching Buddhist teachings and practices very literally or legalistically	
4	**Sense desire**	Remaining habitual craving	First weakened, then broken together
5	**Ill will**	Remaining habitual aversion	
6	**Craving for fine-form existence**	Subtlest forms of craving for refined and blissful states of superconsciousness	Broken together = full awakening
7	**Craving for non-form existence**		
8	**Conceit**	Tendency to compare self with others	
9	**Agitation**	Very subtle tendency to distraction	
10	**Delusion**	Its final remnant	

The third fetter is the tendency that we have, under the sway of delusion, to define things and then take the definition literally, in a way that fixes them. The main thing that we fix is our own supposed self or ego-core, but we can fix anything at all. Fixing is a major element of the way in which delusion operates. For example, we may go around telling people 'I am a chartered accountant,' and really believe that we *are* a chartered accountant, that 'chartered account-antness' somehow defines our being, for no better reason than that this happens to be our job. But really, nobody is a chartered account-ant, teacher, shop assistant, mother, or anything else that can be defined, fixed, and finalized in this way.

The same applies equally to being a Buddhist, if we regard this as a kind of fixed identity. For Buddhists, a major obstacle that arises from this fetter is the tendency to take Buddhist teachings and prac-tices literally or legalistically. This is why this fetter is traditionally called 'dependence on moral codes and religious observances'. In relation to the three trainings, for example, precepts can degenerate into commandments rather than be expressions of the principle of skilful action. What we call meditation can all too easily become a matter of spending a distracted fifteen minutes sitting on a cushion thinking about what we are going to do next, rather than a means of enhancing our awareness. And wisdom might just become a matter of reading books about the wise sayings of Zen masters, and repeat-ing them in an attempt to impress others.

The fourth and fifth fetters are sense desire and ill will. With the breaking of the first three fetters, the grossest levels of delusion have been seen through, but expressions of craving and aversion can still arise. This is because delusion is very deeply rooted and tenacious. The stream entrant's task is to weaken and ultimately eradicate all tendencies to craving and aversion, starting with the relatively gross ones of sense desire and ill will. This involves constant vigilance and awareness, in order to spot such impulses as they arise and well before they get to the point of active expression. At the same time, a stream entrant is always applying insight – from which he or she is now never separate – to every single experience, every impulse and other mental state that occurs. In this way, insight constantly deep-ens, and as a result – ultimately – the fetters of sense desire and ill will are completely broken.

As we saw earlier, full entry into the way of wisdom does not mean that the stream entrant has finished with the trainings of skilful action and meditation. On the contrary, he or she practises them in an incomparably more effective and skilful way, because they now spring from a basis of wisdom. The way of meditation now consists in the cultivation of ever deeper insight, while the way of skilful action is concerned with bringing wisdom into all aspects of life and activity. In this way, the remaining five fetters are ultimately broken – simultaneously, like the first three.

The sixth and seventh fetters represent the eradication of the very subtlest forms of craving – desire for the extremely refined and blissful states of higher absorption that the young Siddhartha realized were not the way to awakening. The eighth is the eradication of conceit. For us ordinary unawakened beings, conceit takes the form of comparing ourselves with others, either favourably or unfavourably: 'I'm stronger than him,' 'She's so much cleverer than me.' It can also take the form of thoughts such as 'I'm just as good as anybody else' or 'Nobody is better than me.' For somebody who has already broken the first five fetters, conceit would, of course, take a much more subtle form. Perhaps it would just be a tendency to think of ourselves as having reached a particular stage of spiritual progress and so implicitly 'more' or 'less' advanced than others.

The ninth fetter is agitation. Again, this would not be the kind of agitation we might feel if we were bored or restless, but an occasional and very subtle tendency to distraction. The final fetter is delusion itself, though what remains at this point is in effect only its final remnant, which is about to be eliminated for good.

7

THE TEACHINGS ON WISDOM

THE TEACHINGS ON WISDOM, and by extension the whole of Buddhism, have one purpose: to enable us to root out delusion and all its effects. Taking words and concepts as far as they will go, they point to the nature of our delusion and the nature of things as they really are, in order to reveal their incompatibility. These analyses are then developed as objects of reflection and contemplation in insight meditation. This chapter looks at some of the more important kinds of wisdom teaching.

WAYS OF LOOKING AT REALITY

Two of the main ways in which we process and make sense of our experience are by plotting things in space and in time. These two dimensions provide useful reference points for our ordinary, immediate experience, and much of the terminology we use to describe or explain things puts them in a spatial or a temporal perspective, or a combination of both. Consequently, Buddhist teachings on wisdom commonly use one or other of these perspectives, pointing us towards the way things really are according to either a spatial or a temporal model or metaphor. However, like all the Buddhist teachings, this distinction is only provisional and expedient: as we progress along the way of wisdom, we begin to pass beyond the apparent duality of space and time.

At this introductory stage, though, it can be helpful to group the basic teachings on wisdom according to these two approaches. The teachings that use a more temporal perspective are those of impermanence and conditioned arising. Those which take the more spatial approach are emptiness and 'not-self'.

TEMPORAL MODELS OF REALITY

Impermanence

Permanence is not a quality that we ever experience, but this doesn't prevent us believing in it, especially in relation to things to which we are attached. Whatever or whoever the object of our attachment may be, we cannot quite bring ourselves to believe that we are ever going to be without him, her, or it. We know very well, in a glib sort of way, that 'things do change' and that 'nothing lasts for ever' – and yet we behave, almost always, as though exactly the opposite was the case. As we have already seen, this is one of the principal ways in which we create suffering for ourselves.

Of all possible objects of attachment, that to which we are most powerfully attached is ourself. We cling to what we conceive of as 'our' body and 'our' personality, and most of the time we prefer not to think about the effects of impermanence upon ourselves: of ageing, infirmity, and illness. Most especially, we do not like to think about the inevitability of death. We are constantly creating stratagems to paper over the cracks of impermanence. We quickly replace worn-out or mislaid objects so that we hardly notice how such things are forever disappearing. This sleight of hand is rather more difficult to achieve with possessions that we value highly, even more so with other people. If a precious possession is lost, stolen, or destroyed, we may have to come to terms – or, quite possibly, *fail* to come to terms – with the fact that it is gone for ever. But when someone very close to us dies, or perhaps a serious illness or accident forces us to acknowledge the inevitability and unavoidability of our own death, we cannot simply shrug off the message that the universe is giving us: impermanence is an unavoidable fact of existence.

What is more, impermanence is not just one fact of existence among many others: it is the very nature of existence. Permanent – that is, unchanging – things cannot exist because, in order for a thing to be unchanging, it would need somehow to exist with absolutely no relation to anything else; otherwise there would be an interaction, and so change. By definition, such an unrelated thing could never be known, seen, or experienced in any way – so in what sense could it be said to exist? To exist is, in effect, to change; without process – impermanence – there could be no existence.

The idea of permanence is just that: an idea, a construct of the mind. It is just one example of the mind's endless capacity to conceive of things or situations which do not or cannot exist, and then believe them to be real. In reality, we and the universe as a whole only exist, and only can exist, by virtue of impermanence and change. We are constant process. The more mindful and aware we are of our experience, the more we see that this is so. All things continually interrelate, merge, separate, and change. Some changes are sweeping and dramatic, some slow and imperceptible; but, nevertheless, things inexorably change. Unchanging, permanent things exist only in our fantasies and wishful thinking.

Conditioned Arising and Karma
A rather more subtle expression of things as they are in temporal terms is the teaching of conditioned arising. In the Buddhist use of the term, a thing is 'conditioned' if it depends on other things or events for it to come into existence, and if its existence itself then leads to, or is part of the conditioning process for, the arising of other things or events. If something is conditioned, it is by definition impermanent, and if the factors which condition it cease, it too must cease.

One of the Buddha's central realizations at the time of his awakening – at least, as reduced to the level of concepts and words – was that everything without exception arises conditionally in this way. This means that nothing exists in its own right and everything is, ultimately, interconnected – one of the most inspiring truths that Buddhism offers us. Everything that arises depends on innumerable conditioning factors and remains momentarily before passing away, having itself helped to bring about subsequent things or events. This principle of conditioned arising applies to anything and everything in the universe. Indeed, the universe itself, according to Buddhist cosmology, arises or evolves in dependence on the ending of a previous universe.

The classic exposition of conditioned arising takes two main forms. One is a bald statement of the principle: 'This being, that becomes, from the arising of this, that arises; this not being, that does not become, from the ceasing of this, that ceases.' Simply hearing this was sufficient for some of the Buddha's immediate disciples to understand the spiritual point and, in a number of cases, to develop insight on the spot. That this principle of conditioned arising was at the heart of the Buddha's awakening may at first seem rather strange – it does not have an obviously spiritual significance. However, the early Buddhist scriptures spell out its spiritual implications particularly clearly in their account of the process of conditioned arising, which is the second main form in which the Buddha explained the principle. In this more detailed analysis, the conditionality process is usually divided into twelve links, or stages (in Pali, *nidanas*). We will not go through these links in detail here, but just survey the main principles.

In particular, the teaching of conditioned arising provides one of the main theoretical foundations of the Buddhist doctrine of rebirth. Buddhism treats rebirth, like impermanence, simply as part of the way things are. According to the earliest records, on the night of his awakening the Buddha realized the truth of rebirth directly, recollecting his own previous lives in great detail, and seeing how all other beings had also lived innumerable previous lives.

The key difference between the Buddhist view of rebirth and those of other religions is that it does not include any notion of a 'soul' in the sense of something fixed and permanent that passes from one existence to another. The nature of what is reborn should become clearer as we explore conditioned arising and the other wisdom teachings, in particular that of not-self.

In common with all Buddhist teachings, the twelve-link formula of conditioned arising has a pragmatic purpose – to help us towards awakening. For this reason, it doesn't attempt to account for all possible forms of conditioning, but concentrates on two crucial aspects: the processes by which we perpetuate ignorance – i.e. the delusion of a really existing self – and those by which ignorance can be overcome and replaced by wisdom.

It therefore starts with delusion – our ignorance of the way things really are. Because of this, in all our past lives, just as in this one, we have acted with a mixture of skilful and unskilful motivations. What has predisposed us towards our present birth is specifically our *volitional* actions, those that are consciously willed and involve ethical decisions. These have conditioned the circumstances into which we were born and the faculties we were born with. These faculties include the nature of our senses and the kinds of feelings we get from our sense experiences.

According to Buddhism, human beings generally experience pleasant, painful, and neutral feelings from their sense experiences in roughly equal amounts. These feelings are not an expression of our delusion; rather, they are a natural product of the kind of psychophysical being that we are. Feelings in themselves are not a problem. If we can enjoy a pleasurable experience – such as eating a delicious chocolate truffle without craving more – or if we can feel the pain of an illness without becoming miserable or fearful, we are not creating suffering for ourselves. If we were able to do this all the time – just allowing our sense experiences and feelings to come and go without any craving or aversion at all – delusion would no longer be operative and we would be awakened.

However, our delusion is usually all too operative. Because of this, experiencing a feeling is almost tantamount to acting upon it – or just reacting to it – without more than a moment's reflection or consideration. So, if a truffle, or anything else, gives us a pleasant feeling, we immediately conceive a 'thirst' or craving for it: we want more of it – in fact, at that moment we'd be happiest if it could last for ever. We are completely unaware, in our rather blind obsessiveness, that the very essence of pleasure is the way it arises, reaches a certain peak, and then passes away. So, from this strong volition of craving, we pass instantly and almost imperceptibly into grasping, meaning that we try to cling to the object of pleasure.

Such an attempt is doomed to failure every time – because, in reality, there is nothing for us to hold on to. To try to cling on to change or process and to stop it is, from the perspective of an awakened person, pure insanity. In fact, the Buddha is once supposed to have commented that 'all normal people are mad' (by 'normal people' he meant those who have not yet realized irreversible insight). It's as if we were to see someone sitting by a river, trying to stop the water by clutching at it. But, in less obvious, much more devious and sophisticated ways, this is what we are all doing all the time: trying to cling to the flowing stream of life. This kind of clinging, which arises from craving, is completely pointless. But this does not stop us from doing it, again and again.

To summarize the process so far, out of ignorance we have acted in ways that gave rise to our present body, mind, and senses. Because of these, feelings arise which are pleasant, painful, or neutral.

Pleasant feelings lead us to crave more pleasure, and craving pleasure leads us to grasp at the objects of pleasure.

What follows from this is 'becoming'. As a result of our volitions in our present life, skilful as well as unskilful, we develop particular tendencies in our being and consciousness. These tendencies, overall, are what make us the particular kind of person that we are. This is known as *karma*. Karma – literally 'action' – is specifically *volitional* action which, by virtue of its skilfulness or unskilfulness, forms or determines what sort of person we become. What we become is not fixed or predetermined: we are constantly changing ourselves through the kinds of volition to which we give expression, whether we are fully aware of these volitions or not.

When we die, it is the *overall* nature of our karma that is the main factor in conditioning the form and place of our rebirth, or re-becoming. And in our next life, we go and do it all again, die, get reborn again, and so on. We could continue like this without end, going round and round in the unsatisfactory cycle of unawakened existence. Unless, that is, we break out.

By far the most crucial of the twelve links is that between feeling and craving. Craving and grasping are the principal ego-forming volitions – the volitions by which we perpetuate our delusion and thus remain unawakened. Our equal but opposite reactions to painful feelings – aversion or hatred, leading to revulsion or repulsion – are themselves mainly the result of frustrated craving.

But although this link is crucial because it shows how we reinforce our delusion, it is also, even more crucially, the weakest point of the chain. We do not *have* to pass from feeling to craving. If we are aware enough, and determined enough, we can experience feelings without slipping into craving or aversion. This is the nub of the spiritual life: to allow ourselves to feel – and enjoy – pleasant feelings that arise, and to be patient with unpleasant ones, but not to engender craving or aversion in relation to those feelings. And the more consistently we can do this, the less we are bound by delusion, and the further we can explore a quite different sphere of conditionality – one in which we pass from skilful states to insight and, ultimately, to awakening itself.

The teaching of conditioned arising means that there is no need, or excuse, to think of ourselves as passive victims of our conditioning, in any sense of the word. Whoever we are and whatever our circumstances or past actions, we can still determine what we become. We can do this precisely because our nature is not fixed and because we are conditioned and impermanent beings. This principle underlies the three trainings, in which we deliberately set out to cultivate skilful mental states and actions, and eradicate unskilful mental states and actions. If we were fixed and not conditioned, it would be impossible for us to awaken. Thanks to impermanence and conditionality, we can all become Buddhas.

The potential for radical change is dramatically illustrated by the popular tale of the great eleventh-century Tibetan tantric meditator and teacher Milarepa. In his youth, influenced by his bitter and vengeful mother, he used black magic to kill a large number of relatives. Such extremely unskilful action would normally lead him to be reborn in a state of extreme suffering; the only way to avoid this, Milarepa realized, was to become fully awakened within his present lifetime. Fortunately, he met a guru, Marpa, who was probably the only person in Tibet capable of helping Milarepa to purge himself of his unskilfulness. Under Marpa's guidance, Milarepa overcame the worst effects of his actions and then, as instructed, went off to meditate, completely alone.

For many years, Milarepa lived in caves and other remote, inaccessible places, unconcerned by harsh privations and totally intent upon awakening. So strong was his determination and so intense his meditation that eventually he realized his goal. After this, though he never ceased to be an ascetic cave-dwelling *yogin*, he travelled much of Tibet, teaching by means of spontaneous songs of awakening and attracting innumerable disciples, many of whom realized very high levels of insight themselves.

SPATIAL MODELS OF REALITY

Before we look at the teachings on wisdom that use spatial models, it is worth remembering that – just as we need to use both space and time to make sense of our immediate experience – we need both these perspectives in order to gain the clearest picture of reality as a whole. Each helps to minimize misunderstandings that could arise from taking the other perspective in isolation.

For example, we could misunderstand the temporal model if we took statements such as 'things change' the wrong way. The potential for misunderstanding is inherent in the nature of language (see page 14). We all too easily assume that to *name* something is to understand it, whereas all we are really doing is making a certain arrangement of sounds that we and others agree can refer to that thing. So if we read 'Buddhism teaches that all things are impermanent,' we may well understand some of the significance of the idea of *change* but assume that the *things* which are said to change are, in themselves, real entities. 'Things', however, is just another word – and we now have to come to terms with the fact that, from the point of view of wisdom (which, of course, is not really a point of view at all), no 'thing' exists. This is where the spatial teachings such as emptiness and 'not-self' come into their own.

Emptiness

In historical terms, the teaching of emptiness developed later than that of not-self – at least in the forms described here. However, although both teachings point to the same basic truths, emptiness can provide a more general critique of the way we tend to see things, whereas not-self helps us to apply the principle more directly to our own existential situation. But this is just one way of looking at these teachings; either can be applied in a general or a more personal way.

Emptiness (or voidness, from the Sanskrit *shunyata*) is a quality that characterizes all things whatsoever. This brings us straight to the Buddhist critique of 'things'. Emptiness is not some quality that is added on to things: it is their very nature. Just as to exist is to change, so to exist is also to be empty. As this suggests, change – impermanence or conditionality – and emptiness are not two different things, but two different ways of understanding how things really are.

When we experience ourselves, as well as people and things in the world around us, we inevitably have a sense of them existing as objects which are 'really themselves'. A chair seems to exude substantial 'chairness' – despite our knowledge that a couple of minutes' work with an axe could convert it into a pile of firewood. So the sense of real, substantial existence does not somehow reside in things themselves, but is projected on to them by us. Seeing them in this way is what makes them seem graspable. The illusion is particularly compelling when we are emotionally involved – we want to feel we can 'hang on' to our loved ones, our dearest possessions, our self-identity.

If there are no things, in the sense of some unchanging, substantial essence, what is there? The teaching of impermanence gave us the clue: there is just process or flux. If, for example, we set light to the pile of firewood that was formerly a chair, what happens is that the 'firewood', as we have now identified it, processes into what we call 'ash'. This process is not happening to some thing which somehow exists alongside, with, in, or behind the 'wood to ash process'; rather, what we tend to regard as 'the thing to which the change is happening' is no more and no less than the process of change itself.

So emptiness does not mean some sort of blank space or nothingness, nor is it some kind of ultimately existing metaphysical quality. It is not a thing in itself at all, but simply a word that indicates something about the way in which any thing exists. What exists is not a thing in any substantial sense – what exists is, as we have seen, just process; and our names for things can be thought of as useful devices for 'locating' different stages of the process. Just as permanence is an idea, a construct of the mind, which we then believe to exist, so ideas like substantiality, true existence, and ultimate existence are all conceptual constructs which have no corresponding reality. If we think of things as having these qualities – and we do all the time – then we misunderstand their nature completely. We fail to see them as they really are.

The teaching of emptiness is not, however, suggesting that the things we try to grasp have absolutely no existence at all. This is a common misconception both of this teaching and of not-self. Something not being *ultimately* real or not *ultimately* existing is entirely different from its not having *any* reality or not existing *at all*. A chocolate truffle is not (necessarily) just a figment of our wishful imagination. Insight into emptiness, then, arises when we realize that there is 'no thing' whatever that we can successfully crave and grasp; like the river, it will simply slip through our fingers. And – the good news – the same is true of the things that we fear or dislike.

'Not-Self' and the Middle Way

The term 'not-self' is a literal rendition of the Sanskrit word *anatman*. It could also be rendered, less literally, as 'insubstantiality' or 'selflessness'. The teaching of not-self is often regarded as one of the more difficult and even problematic Buddhist teachings, but it need not be if we steer clear of the kinds of misconception already mentioned in relation to emptiness.

Historically, the *atman* was a very subtle metaphysical self-entity taught by some of the Buddha's contemporaries, and now enshrined in certain aspects of Hinduism. According to the Buddha, all things without exception are characterized by the absence of *atman* – that is, he taught *anatman* (the prefix *an-* indicating negation). The Buddha's explicit refutation of the *atman* teaching suggests that he considered it a major barrier to awakening. However, most people in the Buddha's own time had probably not heard of the teaching of *atman*, and this must be true for the vast majority ever since. In teaching *anatman*, then, the Buddha was not just engaging in a polemic against the religious views of some of his contemporaries, but pointing to a particular example of a universal human tendency. The teaching of not-self addresses the foremost expression of delusion, our self-view.

We may not consciously think in terms of having a permanent self, soul, or person (let alone an *atman*), but we do act as if we have, or essentially are, such an entity. We have a strong, common-sense feeling that, while our appearance may change, we have or are an essential nature – 'me' – *to* which changes happen. So 'my' body may change, 'my' mental states may change, but these are just things that are happening to 'me'.

The Buddha taught that 'self' is another fabrication of our minds, like permanence, true existence, or ultimate existence. We need to be clear about what the Buddha did – and did not – mean by 'self' in this context. In human terms, he was refuting the assumption that somehow there is something about things, particularly things that we regard as 'me', 'myself', or 'mine', that can be had, kept, identified with, or held on to.

As we saw in the section on emptiness, in reality, all things – including ourselves – have no such underlying self, substance, or ultimate reality. However, it is important to note that not-self does not mean that our experience of our personality is invalid, or that we are somehow non-existent. The self that is being refuted in the not-self teaching is only the supposedly independently existing self that we implicitly think we have or are. Our personality does exist, but it does not exist as an ultimately real thing – rather, like all things, it is a process, a stream of conditions. Consequently, there is nothing about it that can be truly grasped or ultimately held on to. It is grasping at a self that is the manifestation of delusion, and which inevitably leads to suffering.

The Buddha's insight into the nature of self can also be understood in terms of the middle way. In principle, the middle way is the way that transcends a polarity of extreme views. This principle operates in many aspects of Buddhist teaching and practice, but perhaps its most important application is to the beliefs held by unawakened beings about the nature of the self. These beliefs typically polarize around the two extreme views of eternalism and nihilism.

Eternalism is the view that the self is in some way permanent or ultimately real: that there is some kind of innermost essence, true selfhood, or soul, and that this is what we really are, irreducibly and unchangeably. This view often finds expression in religious beliefs, especially those involving some kind of eternal soul and afterlife. In Buddhist terms, eternalism is an expression of craving, in so far as we seek a sense of meaning and security by clinging to self as something that has permanent existence. Such belief is self-view reflecting back on itself, seeking to grasp and perpetuate its existence as a really, permanently existing entity.

At the other extreme, nihilism takes the position that nothing is real, in the sense of there being nothing that we can believe in: all is illusion. This is closely linked to the philosophical position known as materialism, the idea that nothing exists but matter. In relation to the self, this finds expression in the belief that the self is subject to total dissolution at death, which is sometimes referred to as 'annihilationism'. This, too, can be an expression of craving – the craving for non-existence – as well as one of aversion to existence. For example, death may be seen as a permanent escape from everything unpleasant into 'nothingness' – another conceptual construct.

As we have already seen, in their denial of any spiritual dimension to life, nihilistic-materialistic beliefs are no more rational or objective than corresponding eternalistic ones such as the existence of an eternal soul (or an eternal God). Although there seems to be a tendency for atheists and materialists to believe that their position is, by definition, objective, their beliefs have been no more empirically validated than the corresponding eternalistic beliefs.

The Buddha's insight into not-self is an embodiment of the middle way: it is neither eternalistic nor nihilistic, but goes beyond them both. The self – in the sense of the human personality which we experience as ourselves and see in others – does exist, but only *relatively*, not as an unchanging, permanent, or metaphysically absolute entity. Because we exist exclusively as a process of becoming, there is never anything that we can definitively be said to *be*. This may seem a rather innocuous statement; but, if its significance is realized fully, it can cut through delusion – including eternalism, nihilism, craving, and aversion – at a stroke. As a teaching, it brings together both the temporal and spatial approaches to the way things really are.

There is a very important practical corollary to this insight. Not-self is not just something to be known, one piece of information among many others, but is the very essence of the way we are – a way that corresponds with reality rather than an attempt to deny it. The arising of this insight transforms the way that someone relates to the world. Above all, there is a total absence of egocentricity. In other words, insight into the non-existence of the self is expressed in behaviour and actions which are selfless in the usual, colloquial sense of the word. This illustrates a profound truth at the heart of Buddhism: wisdom and compassion are not different things. In developing wisdom, we develop compassion; where there is compassion, there is also wisdom.

WISDOM AND THE AWAKENED STATE

The way of wisdom, and the teachings on wisdom, are concerned with overcoming delusion and realizing insight into the way things really are. But wisdom is not only the path: it is awakening itself. So do the Buddhist teachings on wisdom mean that we can get some idea of the experience of an awakened person from our unawakened perspective? In attempting this, we come up against the limitations of language as never before; but, blinded though we are by our delusion, there are a few teachings that may give us a shadowy glimpse of the reality beyond the veil.

One such teaching is known as the 'four perverse (or topsy-turvy) views'. This teaching enumerates four ways in which unawakened beings misconstrue the universe – and, in so doing, gives us some clues as to how awakened beings experience it. We see things as permanent when they are really impermanent; as having a true self when they are really not-self; as satisfactory when they are really unsatisfactory; and as beautiful when really they are not beautiful. We have already looked at the first three of these. As for the last one, the point is perhaps rather more metaphorical than in the case of the other three. It is not that the things we perceive as beautiful are perceived by awakened beings as truly ugly! In reality, things do not *intrinsically* possess attributes like beauty or ugliness at all. We may find a rose beautiful, and a dunghill ugly; a dung beetle might see things the other way round. Because beauty is 'in the eye of the beholder', it does not have the absolute value – and absolute desirability – that we can attribute to it. There is nothing wrong with the simple enjoyment of what we find beautiful. The perverse view arises only if something becomes an object of craving and attachment for us because of its perceived beauty.

These four views are said to be 'perverse' or 'topsy-turvy' because they embody our misguided attempts to find in the unawakened state qualities that can only be found in the awakened state. As this implies, in the state of awakening we *do* experience permanence, substantiality, satisfactoriness, and true beauty. However, bearing in mind that we are dealing with matters that are really beyond words, we have to be careful how we understand these attributes.

The awakened state can be said to be *permanent* in so far as, once it has been realized through insight, it is impossible to become unawakened, any more than a butterfly can return to its chrysalis and re-emerge as a caterpillar. Permanence in this sense is not contrary to the general fact of impermanence. Awakened beings cannot be said to be *outside* the totality of things changing – conditionality – as this would amount to non-existence. The nearest the traditional texts can get to expressing the condition of awakened beings is to use language paradoxically: we cannot say they exist, or that they do not exist (or, for the sake of logical completeness, that they neither exist nor not-exist, or that they both exist and do not exist.) Maybe all that we can derive from this – other than a headache – is that an awakened experience of conditionality must be quite different from ours. Awakened beings experience it as it truly is, whereas we try to pin it down by using inadequate concepts.

The awakened state can be said to be *substantial*, or real, in a similar way. Awakened people see things as they really are and their actions are completely in accord with what they see. So, although no really, ultimately existing self or substance of any kind is perceived by the awakened mind, that mind itself may be said to have the characteristic of 'true being' or 'the real' – true and real because it is totally in accord with the true nature of things. About this, little more can be said; indeed, even this is too much. Knowledge of the real is a characteristic of the awakened mind alone.

The two other attributes of awakening are, at least on the surface, a little more straightforward. It can be said to be *satisfactory* in that an awakened being no longer acts in ways that give rise to unsatisfactoriness. The real opposite of unsatisfactoriness is true happiness, joy, or bliss. These qualities are inseparable from the awakened mind. Finally, in a metaphorical sense, the awakened state can be said to be truly *beautiful* in so far as it is completely free from delusion, craving, and aversion – the only sources of real unloveliness in the universe.

Nirvana and Samsara

Another traditional term for the awakened state is *nirvana* – a metaphor, as we have seen, suggesting the extinction of the fires of craving, aversion, and delusion. A corresponding term for the unawakened state is *samsara*, meaning cyclic existence, or the round of constant rebirth that we undergo as a result of our fundamental ignorance. Nirvana, the awakened state, is frequently described as 'the unconditioned', whereas samsara is 'the conditioned'.

These descriptions suggest that the awakened and unawakened states are mutually exclusive. Practically speaking, this perspective has advantages: it emphasizes the radical difference between the awakened and the unawakened states, and encourages us to think in terms of progressing from samsara to nirvana. However, the description of nirvana as 'unconditioned', in contrast to the conditioned nature of samsara, should not be taken too literally. As noted in the section on impermanence, anything not conditioned would not exist at all. Instead, this opposite quality indicates that the awakened state is not conditioned by craving, aversion, or delusion, whereas the unawakened state, as such, is entirely conditioned by them.

Non-Duality and Interpenetration

Although the descriptions of samsara and nirvana communicate something of the nature of the state of awakening, they do so – for obvious reasons – from the perspective of the unawakened mind. This perspective is fundamentally a dualistic one. However, wisdom is a faculty which sees through not just the limitations of conditioned existence, but through all dichotomies whatever, including the dichotomy between the conditioned and the unconditioned, samsara and nirvana. The true nature of reality as perceived by the awakened mind is, as we have seen, *non-dual*, and all things are perceived as *interpenetrating*.

Non-duality is certainly one of the most difficult of Buddhist notions to grasp, because our unawakened experience is so fundamentally dualistic that any attempt to imagine non-duality leaves us rather up in the air – we have virtually nothing to go on. We can only approach it via dualism itself. Our experience is dualistic in so far as we have a sense of being a separate, really existing, substantial *subject* over against everything and anything else, which is experienced as other, or *object*. This way of seeing things is inextricably linked to our self-view. All the time we are processing our experience, we are, in effect, thinking 'this is me,' 'this is not me,' and 'this is mine,' 'this is not mine.' This is an important aspect of the way in which we sustain our self-view, incorporating into it whatever we regard as 'myself' (which we experience as subject), and excluding from it whatever we do not regard as 'myself' (which we experience as object).

Wisdom consists in seeing through the subject–object dichotomy utterly. In seeing through our own sense of separative selfhood (the subject pole of the dichotomy) we would implicitly see through the separative selfhood of everybody and everything else (the object pole of the dichotomy). This complete seeing through of the apparent separateness of subject and object is the realization of non-duality. In reality there is no separate anything, anywhere (or any time) – and this includes samsara and nirvana.

There is another way of expressing this same truth, which is to speak of reality as the *total mutual interpenetration of all things*. All-that-is is an infinitely complex conditioning process in which every constantly changing part 'reflects' and somehow partakes of every other constantly changing part. This insight into the nature of reality is evocatively embodied in the traditional image of a vast three-dimensional net consisting of countless multi-faceted jewels – each of them different and each reflecting all the others in its brilliant facets and mysterious depths. To experience the reality evoked by this image is to develop the fullness of wisdom – yet, as we should not forget, it is in no way separate from the reality that we are experiencing at this very moment!

8

THE SANGHA JEWEL

WE REALIZE NON-DUALITY, the wisdom teaching with which we ended the last chapter, when we experience, directly and constantly, our interconnectedness with all things. This is the basis of the ultimate non-distinction of wisdom and compassion. The thought of compassion, invoking as it does kindness, friendliness, metta, and helpfulness, brings us naturally to the subject of this chapter: the Sangha Jewel.

Once, the Buddha's cousin and close friend Ananda came to the Buddha and said to him 'Thinking about spiritual friendship, I realized that 'it is so important, I'd go so far as to say that it's half the spiritual life.' The Buddha immediately responded 'That is not so, Ananda, not at all! Spiritual friendship isn't half the spiritual life. Spiritual friendship is the *whole* of the spiritual life.'

So what is 'spiritual friendship', and how does it differ from our ideas of friendship in general? The phrase 'spiritual friendship' does not really do justice to the idea. In Sanskrit it is *kalyana mitrata* – *mitrata* meaning 'friendship', while *kalyana* suggests 'beautiful', 'noble', 'virtuous', 'good', and a whole host of other positive qualities. *Kalyana mitrata* is the quality identified in the *Meghiya Sutta* (see page 40) as the first of the five stages of the 'heart's release'. It can be understood as both 'friendship with the good' and 'good friendship'. In the first sense, it is a metaphor for the whole Buddhist spiritual life, which essentially consists in the cultivation of skilful states – which are by nature beautiful, virtuous, and good. If we use it in the second sense, it means good or virtuous friendship – that is, friendship based on the mutual cultivation of skilful states. Such rich and subtle nuances are only faintly suggested by 'spiritual friendship', but this rendering does at least help to suggest the link between spiritual *friendship* and the Sangha or spiritual *community*.

The Sangha is – in its broadest sense – the spiritual community of all Buddhists: that is, all those who embody, or who aim to embody, the Three Jewels in their lives. The only realistic way for Buddhists to move towards the realization of this goal is by living in spiritual friendship – *kalyana mitrata* – with one another. This is why the Sangha Jewel is as central to Buddhism as the Buddha and Dharma Jewels. The Sangha is the context in which the Buddha and Dharma Jewels are realized; and spiritual friendship is the medium through which the Sangha fosters this realization.

While spiritual friendship is the lifeblood of the Sangha, the Sangha has taken, and continues to take, many forms; so, before looking in more depth at the nature of spiritual friendship, it is helpful to get a broad picture of what is meant by 'sangha'.

The word itself means simply 'community' or 'assembly'. Although 'spiritual' does not have any direct equivalent in Buddhist terminology, 'spiritual community' serves to distinguish the Sangha from a secular community. Historically, different Buddhist schools have given rise to different conceptions of what, or who, constitutes the Sangha. Just as there are various conceptions of what might constitute a 'community' – for example the community of our family, our close friends, our colleagues, our village or city, the whole world – so conceptions of sangha have focused on different understandings of the Buddhist 'spiritual community'. But before looking at some of the particular historical embodiments of the Sangha Jewel, we can identify a sangha which *transcends* time and space. This is the Sangha Jewel in essence – the Arya-Sangha.

THE ARYA-SANGHA

Ideally, any Buddhist sangha would be a community of people who embody all the qualities suggested by the word *kalyana* – such as goodness, virtue, helpfulness, generosity, and the moral beauty of skilful actions, expressive of skilful mental states. Given human nature, this may well seem an unrealistically high ideal for any community of human beings. But such a community *does* exist: it is the community of all those whose insight is irreversible – in other words, from stream entrants up to fully awakened human beings. These make up the Arya-Sangha, the 'noble community' of those who are irreversibly established on the path which goes beyond craving, aversion, and delusion.

The Arya-Sangha is not to be found in any particular time or location. This community is open to any of us: the only condition for membership is that we realize the Buddha's teaching for ourselves. The Arya-Sangha, then, consists of men and women from the time of the Buddha down to the present day. It consists of married people, single people, and celibates, of Buddhists from all schools and stages of Buddhist history, and from all the very different cultures in which Buddhism has flourished, including today's Western culture.

Quite possibly the Arya-Sangha includes non-Buddhists as well, as it is not essentially an expression of Buddhism as an organized religion, but transcends mundane limitations. Some Buddhists take the view that members of the Arya-Sangha may choose, out of compassion, to be reborn in places where the teachings of Buddhism are unknown or there is no organized Buddhist community. Even if this is not taken literally, it is surely possible for exceptional individuals from other spiritual traditions to transcend at least the first three fetters and become stream entrants.

This does not mean, though, that all those regarded by established religions as 'saints' are necessarily arya-beings. Some medieval European 'saints', for example, were involved with some very unskilful activities associated with the Inquisition. Conversely, it is possible that some people with genuine insight never came to the attention of the religious establishment, or were even branded heretics. However, all this is speculative. In the end, only someone who has developed insight is capable of telling whether someone else has done so; and, even then, they would need prolonged personal contact to be sure.

SPIRITUAL COMMUNITIES AND SANGHA

All Buddhists aspire ultimately to become members of the Arya-Sangha – arya-beings, irreversibly on the path to awakening. But the great majority of Buddhists have not yet developed insight and so need the Sangha in a more immediately accessible form. At this level, it is more relevant to speak not of the Sangha, as if it were a single entity, but of various sanghas. And, while followers of most kinds of Buddhism would probably agree about the nature of the Arya-

Sangha, there is much less consensus about what constitutes a sangha in the more everyday sense. In order to distinguish some of the main definitions we must go back to the earliest days of Buddhism.

During the Buddha's lifetime most of his immediate followers seem to have fallen into two broad categories. Firstly, there were people who – like the young Siddhartha himself, and the religious wanderer whose example had inspired him – forsook their homes, families, and possessions, and became celibate, wandering renunciants. These followers became known as *bhikshus* (male) and *bhikshunis* (female), meaning 'mendicants' – those who, having given up all worldly concerns, depend upon the generosity of others. This was a tradition established in India well before the time of the Buddha, and which still persists to some degree today. These terms are usually translated 'monks' and 'nuns', although these words have connotations that are rather misleading, coming as they do from a very different spiritual tradition.

Secondly, there were those who became committed followers of the Buddha within the context of their responsibilities to family and society. These non-renunciant followers became known as *upasakas* (male) and *upasikas* (female): terms which literally mean 'one who sits near', meaning near to the spiritual teacher – the Buddha or another member of the Arya-Sangha – in order to receive teachings. These are probably best described as 'householder disciples'.

It is clear enough from the Pali canon that the Buddha himself did not make a hard and fast distinction between these groups of his followers in terms of their ability to develop insight. In one Pali text he comments that, once they have developed insight, both groups, male and female alike, 'illuminate' the Sangha. Several other passages show that the Buddha regarded many householder disciples, as well as wandering mendicants, as having entered the Arya-Sangha during his own lifetime.

Quite early on, however, either towards the end of the Buddha's lifetime or in the decades immediately following his death, the situation seems to have changed. While the Buddha's earliest renunciant disciples had been, like himself, wandering mendicants, a new strand began to emerge within the renunciant community. At some point the Buddha started to encourage his mendicant disciples to find a place to shelter during the monsoon rains, perhaps a temporary grass hut or a cave. Sometimes groups of them would congregate together, and in time some of their their patrons built them more substantial, permanent shelters to which they could return regularly. Once such buildings existed, some groups of renunciants began to live in them throughout the year, rather than returning after each monsoon to the more demanding ascetic life of solitary wandering.

These developments were the beginnings of Buddhist monasticism. Eventually, these settled monastic renunciants became a distinct third category of the Buddhist community, following a lifestyle different from that of either the wandering mendicants or the householder disciples. However, institutions have a way of both elaborating themselves and justifying their own existence. This seems to have been the case with the monastic renunciants who, over a number of centuries, established themselves and their monastic lifestyle as the central, definitive institutions of Buddhism. In the process they also effectively relegated both the wandering mendicants and the householder disciples to subsidiary and even marginal positions.

The main role the monastics undertook – and it was a vital one – was the transmission of the Buddha's teaching. This was passed down first as an oral tradition and later in written form, together with an ever-increasing amount of commentarial literature. A considerable part of the monastic teachings concerned the way of life of the settled monastic bhikshus and bhikshunis themselves. This was regulated by an elaborate code of behaviour defined in a section of the Buddhist canon known as the *Vinaya Pitaka*, the collection of discourses on monastic discipline. Some of this material probably goes back to the lifetime of the Buddha, and concerns the lifestyle of the wandering ascetic bhikshus and bhikshunis who lived in the same way as the Buddha himself. Most of it, though, seems to have been compiled during a slightly later period, when monasticism was establishing itself; as a result it is concerned with the principles that this settled monastic lifestyle sought to embody.

Over the first few centuries of Buddhism, monastic schisms gradually led to the emergence of a number of distinct sanghas. In terms of practice, these had a great deal in common, and the schisms were usually caused by relatively small divergences of interpretation of the monastic rules. The main differences can be seen in the *pratimoksha*, or list of core rules, which the monastics of each sangha observe – for example, the 228 rules of monastic code of the Theravada sangha and the 250 rules of the Sarvastivada sangha.

The history of the various Buddhist sanghas has mainly been that of the relation between the followers of the three distinct Buddhist lifestyles: wandering mendicant, householder, and monastic. The details of historical developments are complex but it is nevertheless possible to get a broad impression of some of the varied strands or 'schools' within the Sangha, especially those which still exist today.

SANGHA IN THE THERAVADA

The Theravada school, which is the dominant form of Buddhism in Sri Lanka and much of South-east Asia, is the main surviving inheritor of the early settled monastic sangha. It is the school responsible for passing down the Pali canon, from which its teachings derive.

In the Theravada, the sangha consists of the monastic community alone. Although there is a significant tradition of ascetic wandering mendicants within the Theravada, these function on the whole as an integral part of the monastic sangha. Ever since the bhikshuni lineage within the Theravada died out, about a thousand years ago, the Theravada sangha has consisted of bhikshus only – women within the Theravada are at present unable to become full or novice members of the monastic sangha. Many do adopt a monastic lifestyle, however, by observing ten monastic precepts, and over the last twenty years or so a movement for the revival of full monastic ordination for women within the Theravada sangha has been gaining momentum.

Traditionally, householder disciples were not regarded as part of the Theravada sangha. Their main practice tended to be the cultivation of skilful karma through the practice of generosity. However, this situation has changed significantly over the course of the last hundred years with a significant revival of expectations and serious practice among sections of the Theravada laity as well as many new initiatives within the monastic sangha.

SANGHAS IN THE MAHAYANA

The Mahayana or 'Great Way' is not a single school but a movement within Buddhism which, over a long period, generated a large number of schools and several distinct sanghas. This raises the question of the difference between a school and a sangha. For the present purpose, 'school' indicates a distinct strand of teaching within Buddhism, and 'sangha' means a distinct spiritual community. In the

Theravada, the school and the sangha more or less coincide. But in the Mahayana the situation is a little more complicated, as it would be quite possible for two Mahayanists to belong to the same school but different sanghas – or the same sangha but different schools.

The roots of the Mahayana can be traced back to well before its emergence as a distinct school, around two thousand years ago. The early Mahayanists – most of whom were probably settled monastics – would have been members of existing, non-Mahayana, monastic sanghas. But whether monastics or not, the early Mahayanists were clearly aware of a strong tendency in existing sanghas towards the spiritual downgrading of non-monastic Buddhists. Evidence for this can be found in some Mahayana sutras[8] where, for reasons which are clearly in part polemical, non-monastic householder disciples take prominent roles. For example, in one Mahayana sutra, *The Teaching of Vimalakirti*, the central figure – a mythic creation rather than a historical character – is represented as a householder who is spiritually more advanced than all the Buddha's monastic (and other) disciples, and virtually the equal of the Buddha himself. In another Mahayana sutra, along similar lines, a twelve-year-old girl – a member of the laity, needless to say – unequivocally demonstrates her spiritual superiority over the monastics.

The early Mahayanists were very concerned to re-emphasize the truth – clearly acknowledged by the Buddha – that awakening is possible for anyone, as long as they go about it with sufficient commitment, determination, and energy. One way they did this was by expanding the idea of sangha to include all Buddhists, irrespective of their lifestyle. Just as the Mahayana is the 'Great Way' that everyone can follow to the state of Buddhahood, so its sangha is the Maha-Sangha, the 'great sangha', of all who aspire to Buddhahood. It does not matter whether they are already arya-beings, or whether they live as monastics, householders, or wandering ascetic mendicants – all Mahayana Buddhists are by definition members of this great sangha.

As such, the Maha-Sangha cannot be identified with any particular school or sub-group within the Mahayana. It cannot even be identified with the Mahayana itself in any institutional sense – it simply consists of all those who aspire to full awakening. But within their own particular school, individual Mahayana Buddhists can be members of one of the monastic sanghas, or of a non-monastic sangha.

They can even be a member of a sangha which is neither quite monastic nor non-monastic.

All the settled monastic sanghas associated with the Mahayana schools derive their *pratimoksha* or list of rules from sanghas that pre-date the Mahayana. This means that, strictly speaking, there is no such thing as a Mahayana bhikshu; rather, there are just bhikshus who follow the Mahayana – a fine distinction, perhaps. Also, bhikshus are not the only kind of Mahayana monastic: though long extinct in the Theravada, the female monastic lineage of bhikshunis still flourishes in Mahayana circles.

As for wandering ascetic mendicants, in the Mahayana this tradition often remained vigorously independent of the settled monastic sangha. For example, in Tibet, Milarepa and his *repa* ('cotton-clad') followers were among the outstanding practitioners of their day. Living a classic ascetic mendicants' lifestyle which would have been familiar (apart from the cold of Tibet!) to the Buddha and his immediate renunciant disciples, they functioned entirely outside the formal, settled monastic sangha.

For Mahayana non-renunciant or householder disciples, there have been, and are, many forms of sangha. On the one hand, many Mahayana sanghas embody the distinction between monastics and laity. However, the Mahayana conception of the great sangha means that both monks and lay people regard themselves as members of the sangha in this broad, universal sense. On the other hand, as we will see shortly, some entirely non-monastic sanghas have emerged within the Mahayana.

From these basic constituents, sanghas in the Mahayana world have taken quite diverse forms and directions in different places. Most of the main developments can be touched on briefly by way of a broad look at Mahayana sanghas in Tibet, China, and Japan.

Tibet

The form of Buddhism which took root in Tibet from about the middle of the seventh century was Indian Mahayana, in its tantric phase. At this stage of Indian Buddhism, its dominant institutions were huge monasteries – or rather, monastic universities – which relied for their existence on the patronage of rulers and the very wealthy. Establishing this form of Buddhism in Tibet similarly required royal patronage, and the process took several centuries.

However, though huge monasteries were the most important centres of the new religion, the nature of tantric Buddhism had a major tempering effect on the structure of the sangha in Tibet.

Tantric Buddhism, like the early Mahayana some centuries before, did not make distinctions between householders and monastics in terms of their spiritual capacities. When it came to lifestyle, the great awakened ones of Indian tantric Buddhism – the *mahasiddhas* – were conspicuously beyond the pale in relation to the existing monastic and secular norms. Kings, shopkeepers, and housewives alike became mahasiddhas, while bhikshu and bhikshuni mahasiddhas disregarded the formal monastic rule and became wild, wandering ascetics. The concern of the tantric Buddhists was to practise the most effective path to awakening, rather than worrying too much about the traditional forms and conventions of the Buddhist way of life. What monastics and householders had in common greatly outweighed the differences of lifestyle.

This attitude pervaded the tradition which became established in Tibet. All Tibetan Buddhists shared the Mahayana ideal of realizing awakening for the sake of all beings. Also, most Tibetan Buddhists would have received initiation into a tantric practice of some kind (see page 165) and therefore would have been part of a *kula* – a tantric equivalent of a sangha. Members of a *kula* might be monastics, wandering ascetics, and householder disciples – there was no formal distinction in status. In this tantric context a householder disciple could just as well be guru to a monastic as the other way round.

Until the Chinese military occupation in 1950, Tibetan Buddhism embraced all the three main types of Buddhist lifestyle. The large monasteries – supported both by their local non-monastic communities and by the state – provided lengthy and highly elaborate formal training. Non-monastics and householder disciples could be serious, committed practitioners in their own right. Monastics and non-monastics alike might be part of a floating community of tantric wandering ascetics.

Tibetan Buddhism is particularly well known for its 'incarnate lamas' (*tulkus*), and the fact that many of them are married has sometimes created the false impression that Tibetan Buddhism allows monks to marry. However, Tibetan lamas are not necessarily monastics – nor are they necessarily *tulkus*. *Lama* is simply the Tibetan equivalent of *guru* – that is, in the tantric Buddhist understanding of the term, a teacher who confers initiation into a tantric practice.

China

Chinese Buddhist schools and sanghas are in some ways much more diverse than Tibetan ones. Buddhism arrived in China earlier than in Tibet, during the Indian Mahayana phase. Most Chinese schools are therefore Mahayana but seldom tantric. By the time Buddhism was becoming established in Tibet, Chinese Mahayana Buddhism had already been in place long enough to have developed some unique indigenous forms, such as Ch'an (which later, in Japan, developed into Zen). However, despite the diversity of schools, the structure of Chinese sanghas mostly followed a standard Mahayana model.

Generally speaking, each school centred on its own monastic sangha, whose bhikshus and bhikshunis followed one or other of the monastic rules which originated in early Indian Buddhism. The householder disciples were able to take their practice as seriously as their lifestyle allowed; and, as in Tibet, monastics and householder disciples alike could live as ascetic mendicants. Many, both monastics and non-monastics (though, by definition, not householders), became hermits, living in wild remote places, often as part of a loose community with other hermits.

Japan

It is in Japan that Buddhist sanghas have developed some of their most unusual forms. Initially, Buddhism was transmitted to Japan from China, so most of the major schools of Chinese Mahayana Buddhism have Japanese variants. Likewise, the basic structure common to the Chinese Mahayana sanghas was established in Japan. Some schools retained this sangha structure, but others took a different direction altogether. Zen is such a case. Whereas Chinese Ch'an monastics were of the traditional celibate type – bhikshus and bhikshunis – Japanese Zen developed what might be called a non-celibate monastic sangha, or quasi-monastic sangha. Thus, to be a Zen monk would definitely mean undertaking formal Zen training in a monastery, but this could be done either as a celibate or as a married person. For this reason the Zen monastic sangha is not a bhikshu or bhikshuni sangha in the traditional sense.

Another distinguishing feature of Japanese Buddhism was the emergence of entirely non-monastic sanghas. Shin, a Japanese 'Pure Realm' school (see page 159), did away altogether with the distinction between monastic and householder disciple, the monastics being replaced by a married priesthood – an entirely new development in Buddhism. However, Japanese Buddhist priests (and priestesses) do not function as spiritual intermediaries in the Christian sense, but are more like full-time officiants and temple-keepers.

A further development in Japan, largely a phenomenon of the twentieth century, was the emergence of large 'lay societies', some of which eschew even a priesthood. These mostly derive from the teachings of an iconoclastic thirteenth-century teacher called Nichiren, and the largest of them, now active worldwide, claims adherents in the tens of millions. The hierarchical structure of some of these Nichiren sanghas can be compared with that of modern Japanese industrial corporations.

ENTERING THE SANGHA

This brief look at some of the main forms of sangha reflects only one facet of the Sangha Jewel. To appreciate others, we can begin with a very important question: how does one enter a sangha? This question amounts to: how does one become a Buddhist? Undoubtedly, members of different kinds of sangha would tend to answer these questions in quite different ways. In terms of early Buddhism as represented in the Pali canon, as well as of much of the later tradition, the answer is fairly straightforward: someone becomes a Buddhist by *going for refuge to the Three Jewels*.

On the evidence of the Pali canon, the Buddha happily accepted people who genuinely wanted to become disciples, however they wished to fulfil that commitment. If they wished to become (or remain) wandering mendicants like himself, he would accept them as bhikshus or bhikshunis. If they wished to remain householders or, at least, not to become homeless wanderers, he would accept them as upasakas or upasikas. Whichever the case, the Pali canon records that those who became personal followers of the Buddha expressed their aspiration and determination to follow the Buddha's teachings in the same way, by going for refuge to the Three Jewels – expressed in the following form:

> I go for refuge to the Buddha,
> I go for refuge to the Dharma,
> I go for refuge to the Sangha.

This 'going for refuge' is not just a formula of conversion or an expression of devotion (though it includes both these things). Essentially, going for refuge is the act of orientation towards awakening, or commitment to it, as embodied in the Three Jewels. We go for refuge to the Buddha as the exemplar of the awakened state which we are determined to realize; to the Dharma as the truth about the way things really are and the means to its realization; and to the Arya-Sangha as the great universal spiritual community of all who have realized irreversible insight, from stream entrants to fully awakened beings. It is this act which makes a person a Buddhist. Going for refuge continues from the moment a person enters the Buddhist path to the moment of their awakening, and even beyond. It implicitly embodies a commitment to realizing the whole of the Buddhist path and teaching.

'Going for refuge' may seem, at first glance, a peculiar expression, perhaps suggesting some kind of escapism. To understand its meaning, we can reflect on how the phrase was used by the Buddha and his early disciples. The Buddha observed that it is human nature to seek refuges all the time. Insecurity and fear are unavoidable human experiences, and we are always looking, consciously or unconsciously, for security. In the *Dhammapada*, one of the best-known texts of the Pali canon, the Buddha outlines both the problem and its solution:

> Driven by fear, many people seek refuge in mountains and
> forests, in trees and shrines.

At the time of the Buddha, these were all objects of superstition or conventional religious belief. Such things, or their equivalents for us – possessions, esteem, sexual relationships, career, entertainment, culture – are ultimately unable to provide the security or the meaning we seek from them. In the end, they are inevitably going to let us down – not necessarily because they are harmful or inherently worthless, but simply because of the unavoidable fact of impermanence.

> That indeed is not a safe refuge; that is not the best refuge.

We are like people seeking refuge from a flood in the branches of a tree: when the tree is swept down, we have no choice but to swim about looking for another. But as this image suggests, the problem is not the fact that we seek a refuge as such – under the circumstances it is a very sensible thing to do. The problem with our choice of refuges is just that they are usually the wrong ones.

> One who goes for refuge to the Buddha, the Dharma, and the
> Sangha sees the four truths with true understanding....
> That indeed is a safe refuge; that is the best refuge.[9]

The Three Jewels are the only *safe* refuge because they embody the way to awakening, and it is only by means of awakening that we can finally overcome the existential fear which is integral to our unawakened human condition. Going for refuge to the Three Jewels means reorienting our whole life by aspiring to Buddhahood, by practising the path and teachings, and by participating in the Sangha, in one form or another. It means taking full responsibility for our life and refusing to be passive in the face of insecurity and unsatisfactoriness.

SANGHA AND THE CULTIVATION OF COMPASSION

The act of going for refuge, then, implies association with a sangha. We go for refuge to the Arya-Sangha, as this is a safe refuge – members of the Arya-Sangha can never lose their insight into the way things really are. However, we join or associate with a particular sangha – embodying a particular approach to Buddhism – functioning here and now in the world. But whichever sangha we join, and whatever particular form our joining takes, our act of commitment will, either explicitly or implicitly, be that of going for refuge to the Three Jewels.

Going for refuge to the Buddha and Dharma necessarily takes place in the context of a sangha. The path to awakening is a demanding journey and, with the best will in the world, to attempt it without the help of fellow travellers would make it next to impossible. In fact, the sangha is far more than a means for exchanging teaching and support, indispensable though these are – the existence of the sangha is also a recognition that regard for others is implicit in the very nature of awakening.

Awakening is not like any other kind of human experience – indeed, it is not an experience at all in the sense of something that we do, get, or even become for our own benefit. As the wisdom teachings reveal, to awaken is to reverse the lodestone of our being, from the self-orientation or selfishness which is characteristic of the deluded mind to the other-orientation or compassion which is characteristic of the awakened mind. It is because compassion and the qualities that help to form it – kindness, sympathy, equanimity, and steadfastness – are integral to awakening that the Sangha is integral to the Buddhist path. From this point of view, the Sangha is a training ground for the cultivation and expression of these qualities. Because sanghas consist largely of ordinary people, with ordinary difficulties, faults, and virtues, there is plenty of scope within them for the cultivation and expression of compassion.

This is not to say that Buddhists expect to express compassion only within their sangha – that would hardly be compassion. There are no limits to the scope of genuine disinterested compassion; but at the same time most of us need to recognize that our capacity for genuine compassion is at first very limited. Most of us find that if we have been other-oriented for too long (how long is 'too long' will depend on the individual) we eventually run out of steam and feel the need to 'look after number one' for a bit. So, if we find we are not quite completely selfless, and cannot respond to everybody else's needs all the time, there is nothing amiss. Such total selflessness could only be expected of an arya-being, and a pretty advanced one at that.

Practising compassion in the Buddhist sense definitely does not mean totally ignoring or denying our own needs. Such a course could only lead, eventually, to some kind of mental or physical breakdown, and we need self-metta if we are to cultivate compassion for others. But we need to beware of using 'compassion fatigue', as the popular term has it, as a cover-up for indifference. Within a sangha, there are always means and opportunities for gradually developing a greater capacity for other-orientation, in a wider context of simply enjoying good friendship. At the same time, our practice of the Dharma gradually leads to a deepening of self-understanding – the first glimmerings of wisdom – without which our capacity to help others will really be quite limited.

A TRAINING GROUND FOR
SPIRITUAL FRIENDSHIP

Within the Sangha, we will also find opportunities to develop and explore spiritual friendship – that is, *kalyana mitrata*, with all its nuances. Unlike most other contexts, in the Sangha we get the chance to develop friendships on the basis of shared ideals – shared going for refuge and shared treading of the path towards awakening.

The dialogue between the Buddha and Ananda at the beginning of this chapter illustrates how spiritual friendship and spiritual community work in tandem. Brief though it is, it demonstrates several points about spiritual friendship in the context of the Sangha. In the first place, Ananda was putting forward his own thoughts about *kalyana mitrata*. As he was not awakened, he could not be certain his ideas were correct. The Buddha was then immediately able to make a definitive statement on the subject. More than that, he responded with an important teaching, with practical implications. Ananda knew that *kalyana mitrata* was very important, but the Buddha (after teasing his friend a little – 'that isn't so, Ananda') made it clear to him that he had been underestimating its significance and that spiritual friendship, or association with the lovely, *is* the spiritual life.

The dialogue shows two activities that are important to the spiritual community – clarifying the Dharma's meaning and relevance, and communicating enthusiasm for its practice. The Buddha regarded this as the most useful and profitable sort of communication; and if he ever found his renunciant disciples talking about trivia, he would firmly tell them to either talk about the Dharma or 'keep the aryan silence'.

Any sangha, as a community, consists of a network of two kinds of spiritual friendship. There are friendships between people who are more or less at the same stage in their spiritual development, and there are friendships between those who are at significantly different stages. Both kinds are necessary. Friends who are at the same level of development and experience can give and receive mutual support in the context of similar developments, problems, and experiences on the spiritual path. If one friend is significantly more experienced than the other, the relationship is naturally more that of teacher and pupil, though the basis is still essentially that of friendship. To be a teacher in the Buddhist sense means primarily to embody the qualities of a *kalyana mitra*, rather than having an extensive technical knowledge of Buddhist doctrine – although, of course, the two are not mutually exclusive.

Spiritual friendship does not mean having to behave in some kind of special, self-consciously pious or 'religious' way. In practice it is no different from ordinary warm friendship. Like any other friendship, it can go through periods of being enjoyable, bland, challenging, frustrating, or invigorating. What distinguishes spiritual from ordinary friendship is simply the fact that both friends are going for refuge. But this single distinction makes a real difference. In ordinary friendships, the relationship is often fairly fixed, and personal changes may 'rock the boat' so much that the friendship disintegrates. In spiritual friendship, on the other hand, major changes provide the essential momentum for the relationship as both friends develop their going for refuge. Spiritual friendship could be described as a process of shared, or mutual, self-transcendence – transcending, bit by bit, all the constraints that hold us and our spiritual friends back from awakening.

Spiritual friendship cannot survive without *metta* – the expression of loving-kindness, strong impartial friendliness, and goodwill. Metta is the foundation on which all the qualities of spiritual friendship – and ultimately compassion – are built, and it is essential if our relationships are to survive times of conflict. In spiritual friendships, as in ordinary ones, there are difficult patches – after all, if we and our friends were already perfect, we wouldn't need to be practising the spiritual life. The spiritual life is about changing ourselves, and this process includes facing up to our resistances to change. Sometimes a spiritual friend can see, more clearly than we can, when we need to make certain lifestyle changes, or face certain facts. We might not like them to point this out, particularly if we are very attached to our habits. But if our friendship is based on support for each other's going for refuge, and our responses to each other are imbued with metta, we can work our way through any difficulties or misunderstandings.

This is not to suggest, though, that the Sangha is characterized by continuous mutual criticism! Although helpful criticism, given in a spirit of metta, is an integral part of spiritual friendship, it is only given appropriately and when necessary. There is much more to *kalyana mitrata* – notably mutual inspiration, supportiveness, appreciation, and all forms of encouragement. As in almost any sphere of human endeavour, most people, most of the time, respond far more favourably to encouragement spiced with a little helpful advice than to a continuous battering of criticism softened by occasional grudging praise.

Expressing our appreciation is an especially important and surprisingly demanding spiritual practice. This doesn't mean simply expressing thanks, but also being alert to any opportunity to honour someone else's kindness, generosity, creativity, or thoughtfulness. Appreciation is, of course, the opposite of – and the antidote to – envy and jealousy, which often find expression in harsh, continual criticism or fault finding.

We can cultivate appreciation as a practice in its own right. As we have seen, metta tends naturally to become sympathetic joy when it encounters others' virtues or good fortune; and we can cultivate sympathetic joy in a meditation practice similar to the *metta bhavana*. Expressing sympathetic joy is often referred to as 'rejoicing in merits'. This is often formally expressed in Buddhist devotional practices, but informally it simply means expressing our appreciation to others – and expressing it impartially, which includes appreciation of acts that are not of the slightest direct benefit to ourselves.

A sangha is, in effect, the sum total of the spiritual friendships within it, and operates on the same basis of mutual support and encouragement, metta, and appreciation. Sanghas do not exist as ends in themselves but as a means to an end – the entry of every individual within that sangha into the Arya-Sangha. Spiritual friendship sustains this entire process, but it doesn't end with entry into the Arya-Sangha – in fact, in a sense, this is where the life of spiritual friendships really begins to take off. Someone entering the Arya-Sangha has not only realized irreversible insight – their whole being is now motivated by active compassion. This finds natural expression in fostering *kalyana mitrata* towards others, not just towards other Buddhists but towards anyone and everyone. This vision of the boundless compassion of the Arya-Sangha is prominent in the teachings and practices of the Mahayana, which provides the focus for the next chapter.

9

THE MAHAYANA

WE NOW HAVE a broad picture of Buddhism. We have looked into its heart, uncovering the Three Jewels of the Buddha, Dharma, and Sangha and focusing on some of their facets. The approach so far has been a fundamental one, in the sense of emphasizing the elements of early Buddhism that are the foundation of later developments. Most of the teachings and practices already outlined are derived, directly or indirectly, from the Pali canon, which, as we have seen, contains some of the earliest surviving records of Buddhism. Yet to stop here would be to miss an important dimension – that of its subsequent evolution. In these final two chapters, therefore, we will look at some of the later teachings and practices in which the Three Jewels have found effective expression.

When the Buddha likened the Dharma to a raft, he was partly making the point that a person who urgently wanted to cross the river would put the raft together using whatever materials were to hand. Translated into the terms of the Dharma, this means that wherever (or whenever) we are, we can use whatever means are effective in enabling us to realize awakening. As times changed in India, and as the Dharma was gradually introduced into very different cultures, Buddhism had constantly to adapt to new circumstances in order to remain effective. If Buddhism had not changed, it would have ceased to be the way to awakening.

The need for adaptation was not only brought about by changes to the cultural environment. Awakening, and the Three Jewels, are unchanging in that they embody, unconditionally, the way things really are; but Buddhism, which is 'the raft', is as much a conditioned phenomenon as anything else in this world. The Dharma is always necessarily expressed in particular forms and particular human institutions, and like all conditioned things – including all human institutions – any *particular* form of Buddhism is subject not merely to change, but to degeneration too.

However, if degeneration was the whole story, Buddhism as an effective spiritual tradition would have become extinct many centuries ago. What has ensured its continual development and renewal – the only thing, in fact – is the unbroken lineage of the Arya-Sangha. From the Buddha's time right down to the present there have been people with insight somewhere in the Buddhist world – not merely practising Buddhists, but people who have realized the essence of the Three Jewels. Because of this, they know – returning to our previous image – exactly what, in their particular environment, are the most suitable materials for building a serviceable raft. They can also see quite clearly when the novice raft builders – that is, ordinary Buddhists without insight – have tried to adapt a perfectly good existing design using only the tools of craving, aversion, and delusion, so that the raft sinks shortly after it is launched.

In other words, because the majority of members of any sangha or school of Buddhism have not yet realized irreversible insight, the teachings and practices are always vulnerable to the distorting, appropriating tendencies of the unawakened, egocentric mind – and they are distorted mainly by literalism. As we saw in Chapter 6, literalism is one of the principal expressions of the third fetter, which keeps us firmly shackled to our delusion. People can become fixated on the outward expressions of Buddhism rather than the essential principles of the Dharma. Teachings and practices cease to be treated as a means to an end – the realization of awakening – and start to become treated as ends in themselves. This is not just a danger for individuals; it has happened collectively again and again in Buddhist history, either when there has simply been no one with sufficient insight around, or when those with insight have been unable to prevent it.

We can see the process of degeneration or decline at work in two tendencies. The first is the gradual infiltration of teachings or practices that do not embody the way to awakening; the second is the tendency for sanghas to develop a kind of career structure that reflects people's mundane ambitions rather than the genuine spiritual hierarchy. If these tendencies go unchecked, a sangha can end up a mere husk, empty of any real spiritual aspiration.

Fortunately, people with insight have always been able to keep open the way to awakening – so far, at least. Teachers with insight have again and again guided their fellow sangha members back from blind alleys, or found new ways to teach and practise suited to the prevailing conditions. This has not saved some schools or sanghas from stagnation and even disappearance; but, in two-and-a-half millennia of Buddhist history, the sheer number of new schools, teachings, and practical ways to realize awakening have more than made up for the misdirections. Overall, those with insight – the members of the Arya-Sangha – have ensured that Buddhism has spread, proliferated, and adapted according to need, and so remained spiritually vital. Indeed, it is this very diversity, as well as its lack of a centralized hierarchical structure (in the merely clerical sense), that has ensured Buddhism's survival and continuing spiritual vitality right up to the present.

The way that reappraisal and reform has happened in Buddhism is quite different from approaches more familiar to Westerners. For example, in reforming Christianity in the sixteenth century, Martin Luther and the other European Protestants had to depend on the existing texts of the Bible, as these were regarded as the sole and literal repository of truth for all time. Buddhism, however, depends for its spiritual authenticity not on the literal historical accuracy of any of its written accounts, but purely on the efficacy of their teachings in enabling people to realize awakening.

This means that it is quite possible for reform in Buddhism to be manifested through new canonical texts – canonical in the crucial sense that they embody the essential principles of the Three Jewels, regardless of when or where they appear. At times, not surprisingly, there have been disagreements between schools as to what is genuinely canonical; but this potential open-endedness of the canon is one reason for the extraordinary variety of forms and schools of Buddhism.

Today, there are broadly two kinds of Buddhism in existence: Theravada, which is the tradition of Sri Lanka, Thailand, Burma, and Cambodia; and the many kinds of Mahayana Buddhism, which until recently flourished mainly in China, Japan, Korea, Vietnam, Tibet, and Mongolia. Needless to say, recent political developments have meant that Buddhism is now no longer flourishing in some of its traditional homelands.

In identifying Buddhist traditions as Theravada or Mahayana, we are not really comparing like with like. The Theravada is a single school of Buddhism, even though there are culturally specific variations. The Theravada bhikkhu[10] sangha is essentially unified, even though it consists of a number of mutually exclusive ordination lineages. The Mahayana, on the other hand, is not a single distinctive school in the same sense, but a wide spectrum of schools and sanghas which vary much more widely – and sometimes wildly – than the different national expressions of Theravada.

Within the Mahayana there is, as we saw in the previous chapter, a broader conception of the meaning and expression of sangha. Also, where the Mahayana flourishes there is not usually just one kind of Buddhism serving an entire culture, as does the Theravada in, say, Thailand. In Japan, for example, virtually every major kind of Mahayana Buddhism is to be found, including a number of schools that are unique to Japan.

Among the many forms and schools, there are several whose reforms have particularly left their mark on Buddhism as we see it today. The two most influential developments took place within Indian Buddhism. One, the focus of this chapter, was the emergence of the Mahayana; the other, covered in the next chapter, was the development of tantric Buddhism. Important developments outside India included Pure Realm Buddhism and Zen (Ch'an) – notable examples of the extraordinary variety of schools within the Mahayana 'family'.

THE ORIGINS OF THE MAHAYANA

Where, then, did the Mahayana come from and what are its distinctive features? The second question is easier to answer than the first (except in the very obvious sense that it came from India).

Mahayana Buddhists can primarily be distinguished from non-Mahayana Buddhists on the basis of the texts that they regard as canonical. In addition to their own equivalents of the texts contained in the the Pali canon, Mahayana Buddhists include a number of others, known as Mahayana sutras, which they regard as the Buddha's authentic word. Non-Mahayana Buddhists – and today this effectively means just the Theravadins – regard the Mahayana sutras as the writings of later Buddhists, and for this reason non-canonical.

Exactly how these sutras originated is something of a mystery, and probably always will be. Historically, the very earliest identifiably Mahayana sutras seem to have appeared in writing some three to four hundred years after the Buddha – which is also when the Pali canon was being written down for the first time. These sutras continued to appear for some centuries after that, and we now know that, although they all present themselves as a record of the Buddha's own teaching as remembered faithfully by Ananda and passed down orally, some were composed many hundreds of years after the time of the Buddha, in China and elsewhere.

The majority of Mahayana followers through the centuries have tended to regard these texts as simply the teaching of the Buddha. However, in some branches of the Mahayana there always seems to have been an acknowledgment that sutras could be 'revealed' through visionary experience and other means by later Buddhists. Looking at this from a more Western, historical perspective, it is possible that some Mahayana sutras did embody material that was passed on orally, some of which could conceivably go back to the early days of Buddhism. However, the more distinctively Mahayana the teachings contained in these sutras, the less likely it is that the material had such an early origin. On textual evidence, some of the very earliest sutras that contain Mahayana teachings were compiled by inserting one or two 'new' teachings among a lot of others that were common to the earlier schools of Buddhism. Other Mahayana sutras may not derive from any oral tradition, but have originated as written documents. Many of them probably contain elements of both written and orally transmitted material.

Even if Mahayana sutras are not literally the word of the Buddha, many of them undoubtedly contain expressions of the spiritual genius of the awakened mind. These sutras played a crucial role in the reforming process undertaken by the Mahayanists. Each represents the Buddha affirming the essential principles of the Dharma, but in a new and characteristically Mahayana way. Some included an implied critique of trends in existing Buddhist schools. The teachings of these schools are identified as only preliminary or provisional, having been formulated by the Buddha to match the needs and capabilities of the more spiritually backward among his followers.

In a very influential early Mahayana sutra, the *White Lotus of the True Dharma* – usually known simply as the *Lotus Sutra* – the Buddha explains to a large assembly of his followers that he has not yet delivered his ultimate teaching. On hearing this, a large number of followers walk out in a huff because, says the sutra, 'they had deep and grave roots of sin and overweening pride, imagining themselves to have attained and to have borne witness to what in fact they had not.'[11] Passages like this – which are quite common in Mahayana sutras – are not records of historical events at the time of the Buddha, but examples of the way in which Mahayanists criticized their Buddhist contemporaries, hundreds of years after the Buddha's own time.

The *Lotus Sutra* takes the critique further by labelling the pre-Mahayana Buddhist schools the 'inferior' or 'lesser' way (Hinayana), in contrast to the Mahayana itself, which is the 'superior' or 'great' way to awakening. This was a bold claim for a movement which took a long time to become as large numerically as the various schools that already existed. But when the Mahayana did gain momentum, it changed the face of Indian – and world – Buddhism. In the early stages, though, it needed to establish its spiritual credentials; and depicting the Buddha as implicitly voicing the Mahayana's own criticisms – as well as delivering the teachings that were particular to the Mahayana – was one of the main ways it communicated its message. This 'skilful means' helped the Mahayana to gain the acceptance it needed in order to revitalize Buddhism.

BASIC MAHAYANA TEACHINGS

The overall thrust of the early Mahayanists' criticisms was aimed at a perceived narrowing of spiritual horizons. Over the several hundred years since the time of the Buddha, various aspects of Buddhism had succumbed to literalism and ossification. This is not to suggest that, other than the first Mahayanists, there was no one left who embodied the true spirit of Buddhism. This is most unlikely, even though the Mahayana polemically referred to all preceding schools as the 'inferior way'. Buddhism had spread fairly widely by this time (approximately the first century CE), both in the Indian subcontinent and beyond. Indeed, before the Mahayana emerged, the great Indian emperor Ashoka had already sent Buddhist missionaries as far afield as Central Asia and even Egypt. Given the ever-widening geographical distribution of Buddhist teachings and practice, and the fact that there was already a variety of schools and sanghas, there were almost certainly places where the Three Jewels still shone in their full glory.

But although the outlook may not have been gloomy everywhere, some Indian Buddhists evidently saw a need for revitalization. In particular, they focused on the spiritual limitations of the followers of the so-called Hinayana, whom they criticized mainly for being motivated by the wish to be free from their *own* suffering, and to enter a nirvana of perfect quiescence and endless peace, separate for ever from the world. For the Mahayanists, this 'inferior way' was to be avoided at all costs. The Mahayana asserted again and again that the *only* way to full awakening was the 'great way' of wisdom and compassion, whence we aspire to realize awakening not merely for our own sake, but with the compassionate motivation of wishing to lead 'all living beings whatever' to awakening as well.

The tendency that the Mahayana was warning against could be characterized as 'spiritual individualism', a relatively subtle expression of self-concern or selfishness dressed in spiritual clothing. The Mahayana's main way to counter it was to recommend that Buddhists follow the example of the Buddha himself. By this they meant not only the his life before his awakening and his activity as an awakened teacher, but also his previous lives. These were recounted in the *Jatakas*, Buddhist texts which depict the spiritual strivings of the Buddha-to-be, referred to as the *Bodhisattva*. They show his development and exemplification of innumerable spiritual qualities, and above all his readiness to give his time, possessions, and even his life for the benefit of others.

The Bodhisattva Ideal
'Bodhisattva' is a pivotal term in the Mahayana. Its direct translation is 'awakening being', and this is understood in two closely related ways: as a being who is in the *process* of becoming awakened, and as a being who is *intent* upon awakening. In the canonical texts of the earlier Buddhist schools, there is to all intents and purposes only one Bodhisattva – or at least only one in every 'world age' (this being a very long time indeed). That single Bodhisattva, in the case of our world age, ultimately became Siddhartha Gautama.

However, the Mahayanists not only gave their own special interpretation to the term Bodhisattva, but created a spiritual mythology around it. In the Mahayana sutras, 'Bodhisattva' applies not just to the Buddha-to-be, but potentially to any Buddhist. In fact, a Mahayana Buddhist is, by definition, one who aspires to the ideal of being or becoming a Bodhisattva, on the way to becoming a fully awakened Buddha. Equally importantly, the Mahayana sees a Bodhisattva as a person who is not just intent on awakening, but one who is intent on awakening *for the benefit of all sentient beings*. In other words, a Bodhisattva is a Buddhist who never supposes for a moment that it is possible to attain awakening for their own exclusive benefit.

The Mahayana discovered, in the Bodhisattva ideal, a highly effective antidote to spiritual egocentricity. The process of becoming a Buddha is seen to involve all kinds of selfless action, and to take an inconceivably long time – no less than three world ages. This altruistic aspiration is reflected in both the teachings and the spiritual mythology of the Mahayana. In particular, the teachings re-examined the nature of the relationship between awakened beings and the unawakened whose sufferings they sought to assuage.

Earlier schools had tended to see the moment of the Buddha's death – his *parinirvana* or entry into final nirvana – as tantamount to his complete separation from the universe as unawakened beings know it. This applied not just to the Buddha but to anyone who was awakened. Even in life, let alone after death, their essential state could not be described or comprehended, in any way, by those who were not awakened. The Mahayana did not dispute the fact that the unawakened mind cannot comprehend the awakened mind. But it emphasized (or, rather, re-emphasized, as this was both taught and exemplified by the Buddha in the first place) that compassionate action is integral to the awakened state.

How, though, could compassion be exemplified by beings who apparently now dwelt in a sphere of absolute quiescence and ineffable peace, entirely separate from the world of suffering? To the Mahayanists, this very idea of a separate, final nirvana was an expression of subtle egotism and, as such, a wrong view about the ultimate nature of things. Instead, the Mahayana put forward the teaching outlined at the end of Chapter 7: in so far as awakening consists of the transcendence of all dualities, the ultimate duality to be transcended is that of samsara and nirvana themselves. Rather than seeing the goal of the spiritual path in terms of nirvana as a reality 'out there', separate from everything we experience, the Mahayana emphasized that reality is integral, a whole. The state of awakened beings may be incomprehensible to us, but there is no separate 'hyper-reality' for them to disappear into.

Given that both awakened and unawakened beings exist within the only reality there is (however many dimensions that reality may contain or comprise), there is no absolute separation between the compassion of awakened beings and its objects – unawakened beings. Thus the Mahayana sutras outline the career of the Bodhisattva as one of virtually endless compassionate action. They also identify the many qualities needed by the Bodhisattva to be fully effective. These include not only spiritual qualities – above all the six 'transcendental virtues' of generosity, skilful action, forbearance, vigour, meditation, and wisdom – but also ordinary human capacities, such as expertise in the arts and sciences. The reason for this lies in the centrality of the compassionate motivation. Wishing someone well and free from suffering is not enough; we need the practical capacity to do something about it. The Mahayana sutras invariably depict Bodhisattvas as idealized beings whose capacity for compassionate action is literally superhuman.

What is meant as an inspiring incentive could, though, seem discouragingly unattainable. Who could really act like the kind of Bodhisattva who is willing to do *anything* – even to spend an aeon with beings in hell-like states – in order to lead them to the path to awakening? And, with so much suffering in the world, how could even a truly remarkable person (let alone an ordinary average one) do more than a limited amount towards its alleviation?

But this is to take the idealizations of the Mahayana sutras too literally. Their heightened use of language is a kind of confluence between a sublime spiritual ideal and the literary culture from which they emerged, which had a fondness for piling superlative upon superlative. For example, in the Pali canon the Buddha is often described as teaching an assembly of '500 bhikkhus', which seems to be a shorthand way of saying 'quite a lot'; but in the *Lotus Sutra* the assembly is said to consist of 78,000 bhikshus, bhikshunis, and Bodhisattvas, plus 'several hundred thousand' other humans, and around 15,000,000 divine or semi-divine beings!

This tendency to elaboration and idealization is even more marked in the descriptions of the 'pure Buddha realms' found in Mahayana sutras. A Buddha realm is the spiritual sphere of influence of a particular Buddha. Our world is said to be the *impure* Buddha realm of the Buddha Siddhartha Gautama – or Shakyamuni, 'the sage of the Shakya clan', as he is usually known in the Mahayana. It is impure because it consists not only of members of the Arya-Sangha, but of unawakened beings as well. A *pure* Buddha realm is a world where only arya-beings dwell – usually only advanced Bodhisattvas. They are not worlds in the ordinary sense, but planes, or dimensions, of higher spiritual being.

At the heart of each of these realms is the Buddha who has in effect created the realm through aeons of unstinting effort as a Bodhisattva. As such, a Buddha realm is the tangible outcome of all a Buddha's compassionate action, as well as the principal sphere of its expression and continuation after his (or – in later Mahayana and tantra – her) awakening. The Buddha of a pure realm does not take an ordinary human form, like Shakyamuni, but manifests as a glorious body of light, unceasingly teaching the Dharma. The realm is similarly glorious: the trees are made of jewels, the ground of gold and lapis lazuli, and the beings – Bodhisattvas – are all radiantly beautiful and seated on vast lotuses of light. And everything, without exception, reminds the beings of the Dharma – the Buddha and great Bodhisattvas are always teaching, in innumerable ways, and even the wind in the trees says 'impermanence, impermanence'. Such descriptions frequently go on for page after page.

To take all this literally is to miss the point – but so is dismissing it as mere fantasy. The Bodhisattva's endlessly, unfailingly compassionate acts, the vast span of the Bodhisattva's career, the creation of a Buddha realm with all its transcendental beauty, could all be seen as a kind of spiritual hyperbole, an overflowing of image and metaphor through which the early masters of the Mahayana strove to give unawakened people at least an inkling of the truly inexpressible sublimity of the awakened state.

Faith and Devotion

The richly imaginative Mahayana 'style' may seem to contrast oddly with the incisive approach of the teachings on emptiness and impermanence. But the early Mahayanists seem to have been aware that people were likely to succeed in the difficult task of awakening only if they brought *all* aspects of themselves to the path. As we have seen, we are not just rational beings – we have emotional and instinctual drives as well. What's more, to the extent that we are driven by craving and aversion, we are *predominantly* non-rational beings. 'My heart ran away with my head' is a frequent inner refrain (or rationalization) for something we have impetuously and ill-advisedly done, though it's at least as likely to have been our stomach or our hormones that led us.

This being the case, trying to leave the emotions out of the spiritual life, either by denying the existence of our unskilful ones or by not bothering to cultivate skilful ones, is to court disaster. In the context of spiritual development, as in virtually any situation, we respond best when our emotions are involved – and best of all when both our reasoning and our emotional faculties are operating together, in a skilful and integrated way.

The Mahayana sought to counteract developments in Indian Buddhism that had tipped the balance too far in the direction of the rational. The main project of the bhikshu sanghas of most schools in the first few centuries after the Buddha's death had become the development of the *abhidharma* – the 'pure dharma'. This was an attempt to systematize the Buddha's teachings on wisdom in essential form, minus the stories, images, metaphors, and so on in which the original canonical texts present them. Some schools included the abhidharma in their canon, others did not, but it is unlikely that the Buddha himself ever systematized his teachings to this extent.

In effect, the abhidharma texts are simply sets of lists, analysing the various aspects of experience into their ultimate constituents. These lists were originally intended to be used as topics or guidelines for insight meditation: a means of seeing through the delusion of a really existent self by, so to speak, taking the self to pieces – seeing that, in all the constituents of our being, and of the perceived universe as a whole, there is nowhere for it to hide. But even though the abhidharma texts are extremely important and of great value doctrinally, it seems that many of the pre-Mahayana abhidharmists were subject to two major pitfalls.

First, they fell into the trap of literalism: having broken down all human experience into what they could identify as the ultimate *perceivable* constituents, they began to conceive of these as *truly* ultimate entities. Second, they began to regard the abhidharma project as an end in itself, so that the analysis was pursued not in order to cultivate insight but as an almost purely scholastic enterprise. Clearly, these two tendencies are closely related: if people suppose that an essentially rational analysis will identify the truly ultimate constituents of experience, they are likely to rate rational analysis more highly than other activities – especially activities which engage or emphasize the emotional side of our nature as well.

The Mahayana certainly did not deny the importance of rationality in the spiritual life. It continued to develop the abhidharma along its own lines, and in the course of time developed a number of 'philosophical' schools of its own. At the same time, it firmly re-emphasized the value of emotional engagement with reality, especially through beauty, myth, symbol, and image, as well as literature, art, and music. The Mahayana developed all these areas as aspects of the Buddhist path, recognizing their value in integrating heart and head, and in deepening our capacity to understand and respond to human experience.

We have just seen one important aspect of the way in which it did this. In developing its own spiritual mythology, the Mahayana produced works of art of extraordinary variety and power, depicting a magnificent spiritual universe with mind-boggling evocations of the ultimate nature of reality in terms of metaphors, images, similes, parables, and myths. The Mahayana employed everything from simple story-telling to what we in the West call the fine arts: painting, sculpture, architecture, literature, poetry, and probably music too (certainly a feature of the later Mahayana). The objective of all this – although using terms that the original Mahayanists would not have used themselves – was the union of reason and emotion and the resulting emergence of integrated faculties that embody both elements.

One example of such an integrated faculty is the state of absorption needed for effective insight meditation – thought and emotion combined in an intensely skilful, penetrating clarity. Another integrated faculty, one of particular significance in the Mahayana because of its importance in countering one-sided rationality, is that of faith, and its active expression, devotion.

Faith and devotion are essential aspects not just of the Mahayana but of all Buddhist practice: without faith, quite simply, we cannot become awakened. Their importance has sometimes been forgotten or obscured, and they are certainly open to misunderstanding, especially by people coming to Buddhism from a Western background whose preconceptions about faith and devotion are based on their experience of Western religions. It is not altogether surprising that some Eastern Buddhists and Western scholars during the last couple of centuries have deliberately ignored or played down these aspects, sometimes rather naïvely wishing to present Buddhism to the modern, scientific world as a 'rational religion' (which, though true, is not the whole truth). All schools of Buddhism today, value and cultivate faith and devotion.

It is important to be clear what Buddhists mean by faith and devotion. These are never based on mere blind belief or acceptance of doctrines which, ultimately, cannot be proved or disproved. In Buddhism, faith is always tempered by understanding. Although usually translated as 'faith', the original term, *shraddha*, also means 'confidence' and 'trust', and these words are a clearer guide to the qualities involved.

The main focus of faith and devotion is the Buddha, both as the primary human embodiment of awakening and as supreme teacher of the way to awakening. We can develop our initial confidence and trust in the Buddha only by evaluating his teachings and deciding that they seem reasonable. This evaluation is not a purely rational or intellectual process. When we reflect on the Buddha's teaching as to why we experience life as unsatisfactory, we can check it out from various angles of our own experience. According to one ancient view, faith arises out of our experience of suffering or unsatisfactoriness. If the teachings make sense in the light of our own experience, we are much more likely to feel inclined to put them into practice. Putting them into practice then gives us immediate first-hand evidence: do they lead to the results that are claimed? Assuming that they do, we have at least a provisional basis for confidence in the teachings and trust in the Buddha. From this point, the further we penetrate into and realize the teachings for ourselves, the more our faith deepens.

Faith, then, is essential for motivating our practice of the way to awakening. The more faith we have, the more we will be able to practise wholeheartedly and unceasingly, and to go for refuge to the Three Jewels. The Mahayana was greatly concerned with faith – how to engender it, how to deepen it. One of the most effective ways of increasing faith is to express devotion – that is, feelings of reverence, honour, and aspiration towards the ideal, as embodied in the Buddha – through ritual and devotional practices.

Devotional practices originally arose out of natural expressions of respect for the Buddha by his immediate followers. In the Pali canon, followers who approach the Buddha are always described as saluting him respectfully with their hands together, bowing or prostrating towards him, and often walking around him, keeping their right shoulder towards him (the opposite being considered a token of disrespect). After his death, Buddhists directed these feelings of respect and reverence for the Buddha towards places and things associated with him, as many early Buddhist sculptures show. At some point people began to create images of the Buddha which were used as the focus for devotional feelings, as were embodiments or symbols of the Dharma and the Arya-Sangha. One of the best-known forms of Buddhist monument used as an object of worship is the *stupa*, a relic-holder containing remains of the Buddha or of any other highly-regarded Buddhist. These stupas can be seen in various forms in many parts of the world, wherever Buddhism has taken root – for example, the 'peace pagodas' built by a Japanese sangha in many Western cities.

Naturally, faith and devotion towards the Three Jewels were expressed not only by physical gestures but in words – whether as spontaneous devotional poems or hymns of praise, or in a more formalized way. In particular, the chanting of the formula of the three refuges – the fundamental act of self-identification as a follower of the Buddha, practitioner of the Dharma, and member of the Sangha – is the essential Buddhist devotional act. It is not just an expression of respect towards the Three Jewels, because of faith in them, but also, implicitly, of orientation and movement towards them – the process of self-transformation through which we ultimately come to embody the Three Jewels ourselves. Many other devotional chants feature in various kinds of devotional ceremony (*puja*), some very simple, some highly elaborate, extolling and embodying the many facets of the Three Jewels.

The Mahayana's distinctive contribution to the practice of faith and devotion was to find many more focuses for their expression. The Buddha Shakyamuni remained the primary focus, but in addition the Mahayana Buddhists developed cults of devotion towards idealized

or 'archetypal' Buddhas and Bodhisattvas. According to the Mahayana sutras, all these figures were, at one time, ordinary human
beings, but they practised the path to awakening so wholeheartedly
and for such a very long time that they now possess all kinds of
extraordinary qualities. These Bodhisattvas are only just short of full
awakening (but are depicted as having all the qualities of a fully
awakened being), and the Buddhas preside over the pure Buddha
realms that they themselves have brought into being, out of their
great compassion.

The sutras name hundreds and speak of countless billions of these
Buddhas and Bodhisattvas, but in practice a more manageable number became the centre of attention, taking a prominent place in
various Mahayana sutras. These figures can be described as 'archetypal' because each embodies a particular quality or function of
awakening. Thus, among Bodhisattvas, Manjushri ('gentle radiance')
embodies above all transcendental wisdom, Avalokiteshvara ('the
prince who looks with compassion') and Tara ('she who ferries
across') both embody compassion, and Vajrapani ('thunderbolt in
hand') embodies awakened energy. As Avalokiteshvara's translated
name suggests, the Bodhisattvas are regarded as spiritual princes and
princesses – heirs to the awakened state, and this is exactly how they
are represented in Buddhist art – wearing beautiful jewels and fine
garments, in stark contrast to the plainly clad, unadorned bhikshus.
Archetypal Buddhas include Amitabha ('infinite light'), who presides over Sukhavati ('the blissful'), probably the most celebrated of
all the pure Buddha realms, and Akshobhya ('imperturbable'), who
presides over Abhirati ('supreme joy').

Where did these figures come from? In a sense they are literally
what they appear to be – embodiments or manifestations of the
awakened mind. Their probable origins can be traced back to very
early Buddhism. In what scholars regard as one of the most archaic
Buddhist texts, a section of the *Sutta Nipata* of the Pali canon, there is
an account of Pingiya, a bhikshu who is a personal disciple of the
Buddha, but too old and infirm to go and see him any more. He
affirms to other bhikshus that he and the Buddha are never apart: 'I
see him with my mind as if with my eye.... I pass the night revering
him.'[12] Pingiya's great devotion towards the Buddha enables him to
feel as if he is in the Buddha's presence all the time, and even to see
him with the inner eye – not just the eye of imagination but that of

devotion too. Many early Mahayanists also clearly felt tremendous devotion towards the Buddha, and some of them probably 'saw' the Buddha in the same way that Pingiya did.

There is also one example in earlier Buddhism of an idealized Bodhisattva. This was the Bodhisattva Maitreya, 'the loving one', the embodiment of metta at its highest level. He was – and is – regarded by non-Mahayana as well as Mahayana Buddhists as the Bodhisattva who will become the next Buddha in this world. In the Pali canon, the Buddha reveals that Maitreya will take birth here, having come from the divine world called 'the contented', when the Dharma taught by the present Buddha has finally disappeared completely – as it must, one day, because of the impermanent nature of all things. Just as the historical Buddha did, Maitreya will rediscover the Dharma entirely through his own efforts, gain full awakening, and re-establish Buddhism in the world.

Given the breadth and universality of the Mahayanists' vision, it seems very likely (although there is no way of being historically certain about this) that not only Maitreya but other Buddhas and Bodhisattvas in glorious forms simply proliferated in their spiritual imagination, or appeared spontaneously in their meditative experience. Their faith was so strong that, for them, these Buddhas and Bodhisattvas were just as real – and just as effective as objects of faith and devotion – as the historical Buddha was to Pingiya. These archetypes of awakening have inspired Mahayana followers ever since.

MAHAYANA SCHOOLS

Although there are uncertainties about the origins of the Mahayana, we can assume that it probably started with a small number of Buddhists who saw things differently from the majority of their contemporaries, and who gradually acquired a distinct identity. As such, the Mahayana was potentially just one more school among the fair number that by then existed; but the Mahayana did not remain a single school. Instead, its sutras and teachings became the basis for the development of a broad movement, from which there eventually appeared a number of schools. The main ones within relatively early Indian Mahayana were the 'middling' or 'middlemost' school, usually referred to by its Sanskrit name, Madhyamaka; and the Chittamatra or 'mere consciousness' school. Also significant are the Tathagatagarbha or 'Buddha within' school, and the Pure Realm schools. Ch'an or Zen, Chinese in origin, is another important, though slightly later, Mahayana school.

Labelling these (and later Mahayana developments) as 'schools' is a convenience, but they are not all quite the same thing. Their followers would accept all the basic Mahayana teachings outlined above, but the different schools developed quite different emphases – for example, on analytical insight (the Madhyamaka), deep meditation (the Chittamatra), or faith and devotion (the Pure Realm schools). They are not mutually exclusive, and indeed later Mahayanists made fairly successful efforts to weld them all together into a single Mahayana system. Modern Mahayana schools – such as Zen and the various kinds of Tibetan Buddhism – are schools in a rather different sense, though still not a uniform one. Zen embodies elements of Madhyamaka, Chittamatra, and Tathagatagarbha, and the various Tibetan Buddhist schools differ not so much in terms of their doctrinal emphases – all the main ones embrace the teachings of the principal earlier Mahayana schools – as in the particular tantric teachings they hand down.

One of the distinctive features of the early Indian Mahayana schools, in contrast to later Mahayana developments, is that they all arise from, and look to, a particular sutra or group of sutras. We have already encountered some of the basic teachings of these schools in previous chapters, so what follows is a summary of the main points.

The Madhyamaka

The Madhyamaka school looks to a group of texts known as the Perfect Wisdom sutras. These were mainly concerned with the nature of wisdom, and in particular countered the earlier Abhidharmists' view that the ultimate perceivable constituents of experience were truly real, ultimate, entities. The Perfect Wisdom sutras stressed that belief in the existence of 'ultimate constituents', however subtle, will obstruct our realization of the way things really are, since all things are by nature empty of anything ultimate at all. Emptiness, lack of substantiality, is the constant refrain of the Perfect Wisdom sutras. One of these sutras, the *Heart Sutra*, characterizes the nature of existence in this way:

> All things are by nature emptiness – neither coming into
> existence, nor ceasing to be.

This shows a characteristic feature of the Perfect Wisdom teaching: the use of paradox to challenge the simplistic assumptions of the conceptual mind. Common sense tells us that things exist but – as the teaching of emptiness reveals – the things that we suppose to exist are not 'really existing things' in the way that we suppose them to be: hence, no (ultimately real) thing comes into existence, or ceases to be. But even though the statement can be explained in this way, the implication of the paradoxes of the Perfect Wisdom sutras is that the unawakened mind *should* be baffled and perplexed by emptiness because it does *not* see things as they really are.

The Madhyamaka school itself was founded by Nagarjuna, who lived in the second century CE. His most important work, called simply *Wisdom*, is a systematic assault on all conceptual assumptions whatever. For the unawakened mind, to name something is tantamount to fixing it as a really existing entity. To expose this delusion, Nagarjuna adopted a highly analytical approach, using a selection of conceptualizations ranging from everyday things like sight, fire and its fuel, and the experience of time, through to the central teachings of Buddhism – unsatisfactoriness, conditioned arising, the four truths, and nirvana. Just as the *Heart Sutra* quotation above shows that nothing comes into existence or ceases, Nagarjuna shows – using a complex system of dialectical argument – that none of these conceptions corresponds to a really existing thing. In effect, he demolishes not just the normal objects and obsessions of the deluded self, but Buddhism and all its teachings as well – that is, he demolishes them as ends in themselves, as literally existing entities. His approach is itself a paradox, in that he uses concepts to push the mind beyond the limitations of conceptuality and into the concept-free direct apprehension of things as they really are – which is the nature of perfect wisdom. Such was his achievement that further developments of the Madhyamaka school – widespread and vastly influential though it was and is – largely amount to 'footnotes to Nagarjuna'.

The Chittamatra

The Chittamatra school has several names. 'Chittamatra' means 'mind only', but it is also known as the 'perception only' or 'mere perception' school or as the Yogachara ('the way of yoga'), yoga in this context implying meditation. Historically, it developed just after the Madhyamaka, and to some extent represented a critique of that school. The first known expounder of the Chittamatra teachings was Asanga, but he disclaimed credit for them, saying that he received the teachings directly from the Bodhisattva Maitreya. This school was mainly concerned with the exploration of meditative experience as a means of penetrating into and realizing the true nature of mind.

While the Madhyamaka school points to the way things really are by showing that things are empty of real, true existence, the Chittamatra school does so by showing that what we suppose to be objects external to ourselves – things that we desire, things we fear, and so on – are not real, independent objects at all. Rather, whatever we perceive – whether an apparently external object such as a tree or a hill, or a thought or an emotion – our experience of it is nothing but mind or perception, hence 'mere perception'. We do not, and cannot, experience any thing existing independently, totally separate from our mind and perceptions.

Having realized, through meditation, that there is no real, independently existing object, the next stage is to turn the spotlight on to what we suppose to be the perceiving subject. As one Chittamatra text puts it, 'since [consciousness] has no real object, neither can it have the nature of a knower, a perceiver. Therefore, because the external object does not really exist, the consciousness does not exist in reality as a perceiver.'[13] 'Perceiver' here can be read as 'subject'. In this way, the meditator comes to the realization that apparent subject and apparent object neither exist nor can be experienced as separate entities, outside of mind. When this experience of the non-dual nature of reality – the interpenetration of all entities – reaches its fullness, the meditator realizes the ultimate, true nature of mind: non-dual awareness, which is mind in its true, pure, pristine state. To realize this true nature of mind is to be awakened.

The Tathagatagarbha

The Tathagatagarbha or 'Buddha within' school possibly developed slightly later than the Madhyamaka and Chittamatra, and has a lot in common with the latter. It does not have any one recognized founder and probably had less of an independent existence than the other two schools. Nevertheless, the teaching embodied in its sutras greatly influenced most if not all later Mahayana schools and particularly the tantra, Ch'an, and Zen.

The Tathagatagarbha teaching starts from the idea of the non-dual nature of reality. Reality transcends subjects and objects but, because unawakened beings perceive things dualistically, they see reality itself as either a subject or an object. For example, if we see the Dharma as a path, leading to the goal of awakening, we treat it as an object. This metaphor makes awakening something external to ourselves – something towards which we have to progress. Such a perspective is important and useful because, unless we do tread that path in the sense of putting the Dharma into practice, we will never become awakened. By contrast, the Tathagatagarbha school takes the 'subject-oriented' approach, seeing reality – symbolized by the Tathagata or Buddha – as 'within' us. Buddhahood is 'in here', immanent, rather than 'out there', separate. What this suggests is not that we are Buddhas already, but that even in our unawakened state we are not *separate* from reality, from the way things really are. We are totally *within* reality and reality is totally within us, but our delusion prevents us from seeing it for what it is.

This teaching is often expressed in terms of metaphor or parable. The *Lotus Sutra*, for example, tells the story of a poor man whose friend gives him a jewel by sewing it into his clothes while he is asleep. He fails to notice the jewel, and continues to live in poverty. Eventually he meets the friend again and, much to his astonishment, hears about the jewel and where to find it. The jewel represents the Buddha within – our inherent potential for awakening – which has not literally been put there, but is there by the very nature of things. The friend who helps the poor man – ourself – to find the jewel is, of course, the Buddha.

Another way of expressing this is to say that there is something about us, somehow, that has never been *unawakened* – we participate in the true nature of reality all the time, but we aren't aware of this because our mind's true nature is veiled by delusion. A verse spoken by the Buddha expressed the heart of the Tathagatagarbha teaching centuries before the school itself came into existence:

> This mind, bhikkhus, is luminous, but is defiled by taints that come from without.[14]

The 'taints' – in effect, craving, aversion, and delusion – are, in other words, not of the essential, true, luminous nature of mind.

This 'Buddha within' is not something that we – the unawakened, ego-deluded 'we' – either have or are; on the contrary, the Tathagata-garbha is the seed of the ego's utter destruction. This is not to say that the deluded mind is incapable of trying to appropriate the Tathagata-garbha, but we can guard against this by also seeing our awakening from the 'objective' perspective – as a goal to aim for. Neither the subjective nor the objective approach is more true than the other; both are limited perspectives, pointers towards the transcending non-dual reality that is known fully only by the awakened mind – the mind that has fully awakened to itself. We have a long path to tread in order to reach the place where, in reality, we have always been.

Pure Realm Buddhism

The Pure Realm schools were – and are – important and widespread within the Mahayana. These are not so much schools as the devotional cults which grew up around ideal Buddhas and Bodhisattvas and the pure Buddha realms associated with them. The aspiration of followers was to achieve rebirth in the pure Buddha realm of that particular Buddha or Bodhisattva, in order to obtain the best possible conditions for the realization of full awakening.

One of the earliest sutras to embody this devotional approach shows how a devotee may attain rebirth in the pure realm of Amitayus ('infinite life', another name for Amitabha) by practising an elaborate meditative visualization of Amitayus and all the glories of his realm, 'the blissful'. Such visualizations, usually combined with the constant repetition of a line of praise such as 'homage to Buddha Amitayus', were the main practice of Pure Realm followers. However, just as the other early Mahayana schools were not mutually exclusive – and became less and less so as centuries passed – so devotional practice of this sort would have complemented the practice of adherents to Madhyamaka and the other more 'philosophical' Mahayana schools.

This is reflected in modern Japanese Mahayana Buddhism. On the one hand there is Zen, which takes a very rigorous and disciplined approach to meditation. This is referred to as a 'self power' school, because its approach to awakening is one of intense personal effort. On the other hand there is Shin Buddhism, a Pure Realm school which teaches 'other power': we can do nothing ourselves to attain awakening and must depend on the compassion of Amitabha

Buddha, who has vowed to ensure that anyone who repeats his name even once will be reborn in his pure realm. Shin followers repeat the phrase *namu amida butsu* ('homage to Amitabha Buddha') out of gratitude for this. In practice, although the approaches of these schools appear mutually exclusive, many Japanese Buddhists regard them as two sides of a coin and adhere to both sects without any sense of contradiction.

Zen Buddhism

Zen is the Japanese pronunciation of the Chinese *Ch'an*, which is itself the Chinese pronunciation of the Sanskrit *dhyana* – meaning 'absorption' specifically, but also 'meditation' in general. In other words, Ch'an or Zen is the school of meditation. Zen has found many different expressions in Chinese, Japanese, Korean, Vietnamese, and now Western Buddhism – too many and too varied to be detailed here. However, although the practices of the various schools of Zen are diverse and distinctive, doctrinally it is based on a confluence of Madhyamaka, Chittamatra, and Tathagatagarbha teaching, with a dash of indigenous Chinese Taoism.

Zen emphasizes intensive practice of meditation – both tranquillity and insight – together with constant mindfulness. The method for which it is best known in the West, although it is not practised in all schools, is that of the *koan*. The koan is a method for cultivating insight, consisting of a question or short recorded exchange between Zen practitioners of old. In essence, the koan presents us with a paradox that cannot be resolved on the level of the rational mind. For example, beginners are usually given a well-known koan such as 'You know the sound made by two hands clapping. What is the sound of one hand clapping?' Or, 'There is a goose inside a bottle: how do you get it out without damaging the bottle or hurting the goose?' These questions are a means to an end: our rational mind cannot answer them, but our attempt to do so first of all brings us face to face with the limitations of the conceptualizing mind, and then – potentially – helps us to break through into non-conceptual, non-dual awareness – an arising of insight.

What makes this possible is the context: long hours of intensive meditation practice, constant awareness in all activities, a tremendous attention to detail and ritual and, above all, a skilful, insightful Zen master to ensure that the students apply themselves effectively and wholeheartedly. These conditions, in fact, characterize most forms of Zen, not just those which use the koan method. Zen training puts a lot of emphasis on formal, monastic retreat, both for full-time monastics and for non-monastic followers. Paradoxically – and Zen is paradox exemplified – Zen is also characterized by mischievous humour and lightness of touch.

TANTRIC BUDDHISM

IF THE ORIGINS of the Mahayana are obscured by the mists of history, the origins of the tantra might seem to be lost in a thick fog. In the Indian cultures in which it originated historical awareness was not a strong point, and its origins have to be largely a matter of conjecture. It is possible that the early tantric practitioners did not belong to any particular school or sect, but that the tantra – which has Buddhist, Hindu, and Jain forms – developed out of various magical cults. 'Tantra' means 'thread', as in a set of discourses 'threaded' together, in this case referring to the canonical texts of the tantric schools. The Buddhist tantra also became known, at least in its later phases of development, as the Vajrayana – the 'way of the adamantine thunderbolt'.

Elements of magic are present in almost all religions. People who practise magic are attempting, through ritual acts, to control natural or supernatural forces, and bend them to their will. Typically, magic is seen as a means of getting what the practitioner craves: wealth, sex, the destruction of enemies, and similar mundane goals. But it can also be directed towards the good, hence the distinction between 'white' and 'black' magic. In India, certain primitive magical cults and rituals were transformed into spiritual practices. Though there is little concrete evidence, it seems possible that Buddhist and Hindu spiritual practitioners to some extent selected and adapted aspects of mundane magical rites; many of what the Tibetans refer to as the 'lower' Buddhist tantras are certainly more mundane than spiritual. But however it happened, tantric ideas and practices gradually infiltrated

Buddhism over a number of centuries. The process can be detected in some late Mahayana sutras, which include references to previously unknown archetypal Buddhas and Bodhisattvas who later become prominent in the fully developed tantras.

When the Buddhist tantras were written down, their followers generally regarded them as teachings of the Buddha himself (though very often the Buddha in a special archetypal tantric form such as Vajradhara, 'bearer of the adamantine thunderbolt'). In this, they were like the earlier Mahayana sutras, but as literary documents, tantras are quite different from sutras. They are often deliberately couched in cryptic language with obscure images, revealing their true meaning only to someone who has received the appropriate initiation and oral instructions from a guru who has a thorough understanding and personal realization of the tantra in question. Each tantra centres on the ritual associated with a particular *devata* or 'deity', the term used in the tantras for the ideal awakened being who appears at the heart of each practice.

The Buddhist tantra – which we will refer to as the Vajrayana, to distinguish it from the Hindu equivalent – claims to be a path to perfect awakening in a single lifetime. This is in striking contrast to the teaching of the Mahayana, which reckons on three world ages for the attainment of full awakening. On such a timescale, the potential for spiritual progress in one mere lifetime may have seemed insignificant to many Mahayana practitioners. If the objective is to help all sentient beings towards awakening, how much better to become fully awakened as quickly as possible, because awakened beings are far more capable of helping others than unawakened ones – more so even than advanced Bodhisattvas.

Before going further, the term *vajra* itself needs some explanation. In Indian mythology, the vajra was originally a weapon in the form of an adamantine thunderbolt shaped like a kind of sceptre, which the god Indra used to hurl at his enemies. It could destroy anything in its path, but was itself indestructible. Tantric Buddhists took the vajra and applied its mythological qualities to the nature of reality. Reality is vajra-like in that it implicitly destroys all wrong views and defilements, whilst itself remaining indestructible: for how could reality – the way things really are – possibly be destroyed? Some of the great tantric adepts equated the vajra with emptiness (*shunyata*). As time went on, the vajra became so central in the Buddhist tantra that it created a whole network of symbolic meaning. So, for example, the aim of the practitioner of the Vajrayana was to become a vajra-being (*vajrasattva*) by realizing his or her vajra-nature.

In general terms, just as the early phase of Buddhism appears to have emphasized wisdom, while the Mahayana brought compassion more to the fore, so the Vajrayana phase was characterized above all by energy and vigour. This is only a generalization: all three qualities are, after all, indispensable for the attainment of awakening, and we can find them in all phases of the development of Buddhism. But given the Vajrayana's claim to be a path to awakening in a single lifetime, the emphasis on energy is very significant.

This claim on the part of the Vajrayana should not be taken literally. In principle, the followers of *any* school of Buddhism that fully expresses and embodies the Three Jewels can realize full awakening in a single lifetime. But there is no doubt that awakened wisdom and compassion will never be realized without unwavering determination, complete dedication, and ceaseless vigour. These qualities shine through the lives of all those who, whether followers of the tantra or of other schools, have realized the goal of awakening.

The Vajrayana is a world within a world, in that it shares the Mahayana's view of the spiritual universe but opens doors to wondrous new vistas and dimensions of spiritual possibility. In the Vajrayana, the Three Jewels of the Buddha, Dharma, and Sangha, in which all Buddhists take refuge, are also embodied in the 'three secret refuges' of the *guru, devata* (or *yidam* in Tibetan), and *dakini*. Just as the Three Jewels embody the whole of Buddhism in general, so these three refuges embody the whole of the Vajrayana. They are 'secret' in the sense that they can only be known directly and experientially, but the following descriptions give at least a glimpse of each.

THE GURU AND INITIATION

Teachers, mentors, and spiritual friends have always been an indispensable part of Buddhism. However, in the Vajrayana, the central relationship is that of the guru and his or her disciple. The guru is seen not just as a teacher but as a living exemplar of Buddhahood. More accurately, a Vajrayana guru is a 'vajra-guru', who embodies the qualities of the vajra (and so is a vajrasattva, or vajra-being) and who can therefore give tantric initiation.

Regarding the vajra-guru as the Buddha is not simply a symbolic convention. The historical Buddha, Shakyamuni, cannot be experienced directly as teacher or mentor (except perhaps by those who are close to awakening), so the guru *is* the Buddha for the Vajrayana disciple. According to a well-known saying in Tibetan tantric Buddhism, if at the time of your initiation you see the guru as a Buddha, you will receive the blessings of a Buddha, if you see the guru as a Bodhisattva you will receive the blessings of a Bodhisattva, and if you see the guru as an ordinary human being you will receive the blessings of an ordinary human being. For this reason, a potential disciple must resolve any possible doubts about a guru before receiving tantric initiation, or it will be difficult or impossible to imagine the guru as the Buddha. Needless to say, this approach demands an exceptional degree of faith on the part of the disciple, as well as an exceptional amount of integrity on the part of the guru. But this is characteristic of the Vajrayana, which is exceptionally demanding in all respects.

The vajra-guru's main purpose is to initiate and then guide the disciple in their tantric practice. It is traditionally said to be difficult to gain an initiation into a tantric practice. As with any spiritual practice (or non-spiritual one, for that matter) the more thorough the preparation, the more effective the practice. Stories abound of famous tantric practitioners undertaking tremendous privations in their quest for initiation. Naropa, the Indian *mahasiddha* (the tantric term for a fully awakened person, meaning 'great adept', or even 'great magician'), spent many difficult and frustrating years merely getting to see his guru, Tilopa. And after Tilopa eventually allowed Naropa to find him, he put his disciple through a long series of difficult and humiliating tests before he would grant him initiation. Naropa needed such treatment because he was an extremely proud man; but he could take it because he was totally set on awakening and had complete faith in Tilopa.

A similar and even more extreme story is told of Naropa's own disciple, the Tibetan Marpa, who became Milarepa's teacher. Marpa realized that extreme measures were needed if Milarepa was to rid himself of the karmic consequences of his evil deeds (see account on page 111), and so drove him repeatedly to the point of despair by making him single-handedly build stone towers and then tear them down again. Marpa knew that Milarepa had tremendous potential for full awakening – hence the apparent heartlessness with which he treated him before he would grant initiation. Thanks to Marpa's compassionately wise treatment of him, Milarepa became one of the spiritual giants of human history.

These stories are not, however, typical of Vajrayana guru–disciple relationships. Tilopa and Marpa knew exactly the kind of treatment to which Naropa and Milarepa would respond, and they knew their disciples were capable of withstanding it. The guru has insight and compassion, knows the disciple's needs, and responds appropriately. Milarepa did not treat any of his disciples as Marpa had treated him; indeed he told them that it was inappropriate for them to follow such an example with their own disciples. Even so, a vajra-guru may require the disciple to make some tangible gesture to demonstrate their readiness and receptivity. This may take the form of rigorous preparatory spiritual exercises, the making of a substantial offering to the guru – financial or otherwise – or both. The idea of giving money for a spiritual initiation may seem a little shocking, but it is simply meant to demonstrate commitment and non-attachment. Again, this presupposes that the disciple is satisfied as to the guru's integrity.

In tantric initiations, the disciple is introduced to a tantric deity and the *mandala* or symbolic world of the deity. The mandala is usually represented by a two-dimensional circular diagram, which forms the basis for a complex three-dimensional visualization. The initiation ritual might be very simple or very complex and elaborate. This depends partly on what kind of tantra is involved. Tibetan Buddhist tantras can be categorized as 'outer' or 'inner'. Initiation into an outer tantra may consist only of hearing the guru recite the text of the practice. Initiation into an inner tantra, on the other hand, formally requires four separate 'consecrations', and the rituals for these may involve extremely elaborate preparations and several full days for their performance. However, this is a generalization. Whatever form the initiation takes, it is meant to give both guru and disciple a deep sense of the spiritual significance of what is taking place between them as the disciple is introduced to the mandala. As long as this is conveyed, an initiation can take any form. Tilopa, for example, initiated Naropa by urinating a mandala on the ground.

THE DEVATA AND TANTRIC PRACTICE

The devata, or tantric deity, is the ideal or archetypal awakened being at the heart of a tantric practice. Perhaps confusingly, although the devata is a Buddha or Bodhisattva, it is the tantric embodiment not of the Buddha refuge but of the Dharma. This is because, in tantric meditation, the deity embodies the insights that the disciple has directly realized and so effectively represents his or her most direct experience of the way things really are.

As part of the initiation, the disciple is given a *sadhana* to perform. Originally, sadhanas were magical rites in which a mundane deity – something like a demigod or daemon – would be coerced to appear and then carry out the magician's wishes. In the Vajrayana, sadhanas centre instead on 'conjuring up' an ideal awakened being so that the practitioner can identify with and realize the awakened qualities of that being. Sadhanas vary greatly, depending in part on the kind of tantra into which the disciple has been initiated, but most share a general structure and content.

The most distinctive elements of a tantric sadhana are visualization and mantra recitation. Visualization involves creating in our mind's eye the symbolic form of the tantric deity into whose mandala we have been initiated. We then meditate unwaveringly on the visualized image, whilst inwardly reciting the mantra of that particular Buddha or Bodhisattva. Mantras are strings of words or syllables which act as a 'symbol in sound' of the deity, just as the visualized form is a symbol in colour and shape. The mantra of Avalokiteshvara, the Bodhisattva of compassion – *om mani padme hum* – is one of the best-known Buddhist mantras. *Om* and *hum* are known as 'seed syllables', rich in symbolic meaning but impossible to translate, while *mani padme* – 'O Jewel-Lotus' – invokes Avalokiteshvara as embodying both wisdom and compassion, symbolized by the jewel and lotus flower he is invariably depicted as holding.

A Tantric Visualization Practice

To get a clear idea of the processes involved in tantric sadhanas, let's look at a simple example – a sadhana of Vajrasattva. Vajrasattva is an archetypal Buddha whose name literally means 'vajra-being'. As we have already seen, in Vajrayana terms an awakened person is said to have realized his or her vajra-nature and is, in effect, Vajrasattva (or *a* vajrasattva). Vajrasattva symbolizes our potential Buddhahood – we can say that we essentially or ultimately *are* vajrasattvas, in the same way that we 'contain' the Tathagatagarbha or Buddha within our own mind. So we undertake a sadhana of Vajrasattva in order to realize our vajra-nature. This practice is often performed as a preparation for initiation into the inner tantras, but it can also be performed as a tantric sadhana in its own right.

As in most sadhanas, we begin by reciting the formula of going for refuge followed by verses embodying the aspiration to gain full awakening for the benefit of all beings. This ensures that we recall and reflect upon our altruistic motivation. Next we meditate on emptiness. This is very important, because the whole purpose of the sadhana is the development of insight: we must perform it in the light of emptiness and see the tantric deity, however powerfully visualized, as empty of any real existence whatever. If we do not, the sadhana could degenerate into a kind of mental game and even reinforce our delusion, rather than serving as a means to awakening.

Having reflected on emptiness, we now give it a symbolic form by visualizing an infinite, pure blue sky all around us, as if we were floating in the midst of it. The blue sky is an apt symbol for emptiness – it looks like a 'real thing' but it can't be fixed or grasped. Whilst visualizing the blue sky, we try simply to experience its emptiness. Contemplating a symbol in this kind of way, rather than reflecting on a conceptual formulation, is typical of the Vajrayana approach.

Having completely immersed ourselves in emptiness in this way, we now start to visualize the form of the deity, Vajrasattva himself. We do this gradually. First we see Vajrasattva's seed syllable, *hum*. This way of evoking the tantric deity with its seed syllable comes from the magical idea that to know a daemon's 'heart-name' is to have power over it. We then see that the *hum* is in the heart of Vajrasattva, whom we visualize directly above our head. Although a Buddha, he takes the typical Bodhisattva form of a beautiful sixteen-year-old prince. He is pure white, like the colour of sun on snow. He appears out of the pure blue emptiness like a rainbow, or body of light, which emphasizes that he is himself of the nature of emptiness.

Now comes the heart of the practice. We see – and feel – a stream of pure white creamy nectar pouring down from Vajrasattva and passing through our body, purifying us and washing away all our defilements – all our craving, aversion, and delusion. While doing this, we recite the mantra of Vajrasattva, an unusually long one consisting of 100 syllables. By doing this we are, in symbolic terms, realizing our own vajra-nature. We are pure vajra-beings because defilements and wrong views are, and always were, empty. And this is not true just for us. The next moment, we see ourselves surrounded by all living beings, and each has a Vajrasattva figure above their head and is being purified in the same way as we are. This amounts to a symbolic realization that the entire universe is essentially pure and vajra-like.

This concludes the main part of the practice, but there are three important further stages. First, we visualize each of the sentient beings (ourselves included) merging with the Vajrasattva above them, so that the universe consists of nothing but Vajrasattva multiplied by endless billions. Then all the Vajrasattvas merge into a single Vajrasattva. In symbolic terms, we are seeing through our delusion that there are separate subjects and objects – not only are we not separate from our own vajra-nature, we are not separate from anything. Finally, we see Vajrasattva dissolve into the blue sky of emptiness, before the blue sky itself dissolves. Having seen the empty nature of Vajrasattva in this vivid way, we now experience the true nature of reality directly: letting go of all dualities and conceptualizations whatever, we simply dwell in the luminous, pure, blissful, and empty nature of mind. This is the climax of the sadhana – although reaching it takes many years of assiduous practice, as with any other means of developing insight. The Vajrayana may be magic – but not in the sense of magically producing results without effort!

This particular Vajrasattva sadhana is, relatively speaking, a very simple one: more elaborate tantric sadhanas involve the visualization not of a single deity but dozens of subsidiary ones, as well as mantras and other formulas. They may include ritual gestures (*mudras*) and numerous symbolic ritual implements – for example, vajras symbolizing compassion, and vajra-bells symbolizing wisdom (though both also symbolize many other things, as all tantric symbols are multi-dimensional).

The Inner Tantra
Many of the deities of the outer tantras are ideal Buddhas or Bodhisattvas who are familiar from the Mahayana: Tara, Manjushri, Avalokiteshvara, Amitabha, and so on. The inner tantras, however, often

centre on quite unfamiliar awakened forms which may at first seem extremely bizarre, especially the wrathful and semi-wrathful deities. Many of these have multiple heads, arms, and legs, and are frequently depicted in sexual union with a consort. These extraordinary forms are a graphic symbol of non-duality at the highest level – the union of wisdom (the female figure) and compassion (the male figure) or, in more specifically tantric terms, the union of emptiness and great bliss.

There are two main stages of practice in the inner tantras: generation and completion. The generation stage is primarily one of preparation, involving devotional practice, reflection, visualization, and mantra recitation. Here the completion stage practices are rehearsed, but not yet performed in earnest. The completion stage itself involves various yogic practices – in the original Sanskrit sense of 'union', which in this context implies the union of all dualities. These yogas are not to be confused with hatha yoga, the popular system of physical exercise; although movement and physical posture are important in some tantras, the completion-stage yogas mainly involve manipulating subtle energies within our body. The main objective is to realize great bliss – an aspect of the awakened mind – and to experience it as conjoined with emptiness, the true condition of all things. At a very advanced level, some of these yogas involve not just visualized but actual sexual union, as a means of accessing the powerful energies involved and channelling them into the yogic practice. However, many practitioners of inner tantra – including, of course, those practising celibacy – do not engage in the sexual practices literally.

The use of sexual union, whether as a symbol or as a yogic technique, mirrors the central tantric idea that awakening can be attained by *evoking* the energies of craving, hatred, and delusion and then 'bringing them to the path' – channelling them into the completion stage yogas, by means of which they are transformed into the union of emptiness and great bliss. But mastering these volatile emotions is both difficult and extremely risky. All the completion-stage yogas engender powerful energies which can be very harmful if they get out of control. When it comes to the sexual yogas, though, for the vast majority of us the risk is more that they will be an expression of ordinary sexual desire and ordinary sex. In this area of tantric practice there is unlimited room for rationalization and self-deception. This is why the inner tantras are always treated as far more esoteric than the outer ones, and need the direct supervision of a guru. A guru would have to be fully convinced of the genuine readiness of the disciple before any kind of higher tantric initiation – let alone sexual yoga – would be considered.

In any case, without readiness most aspects of tantric practice would be a waste of time. Milarepa discovered this for himself before he met Marpa. When another guru readily gave him an inner tantric initiation, all Milarepa managed to do was fall asleep. Maybe the yogas of the inner tantras do represent a rapid way to awakening, but this would mean a rapid and very difficult way, not a rapid and easy way. They are useful only for those who are genuinely ready to benefit from them. For others, they could just as easily represent a rapid way to mental instability – or, given that they are presented as 'advanced', 'secret', 'inner', and so on, at least to the development of 'a self-conceit larger than Mount Meru' (an enormous mountain in Indian mythology). Accordint to some tantras, inner tantric practice was only to be taken up after irreversible insight had arisen. Though this never seems to have been taken literally, it does indicate the extraordinary demands of inner tantric practice.

THE DAKINI

The *dakini* embodies the Sangha refuge. In Indian myth, dakinis are dangerous cannibalistic ogresses who dwell in cremation grounds and other sinister places with their male equivalent, *dakas*. The equation of these strange mythical beings with the Sangha may seem a trifle odd, but in the Buddhist tantra, dakinis – or some of them at least – became regarded as fully awakened beings. This warrants some explanation, but as with most matters concerning tantric origins, assumptions have to be made, and what follows is inevitably a little speculative.

Many of the foremost tantric practitioners in India were homeless wanderers. Much in the fashion of the Buddha's original renunciant followers, they would frequently perform their sadhana in places that ordinary people would shun or fear, such as cremation grounds and wild, remote forests. This was partly in order to provoke ego-based reactions such as fear and self-cherishing and then to confront them directly. This fed into their yogic meditation practice – another example of the tantric strategy of exploiting the energies of craving, hatred, and delusion in the service of insight.

Naturally enough, because tantric practitioners sought out cremation grounds, they also encountered dakinis. Perhaps they invoked fearsome beings in order to increase the sense of ego-clinging, which they could then channel into their yogic practices. In any case, by some such process, certain dakinis came to be regarded not as inimical, worldly forces but as sources of spiritual help and strength. It seems that the inner tantras emerged out of the experiences of these homeless tantric practitioners; and in the sadhanas that centre on deities in sexual union, the female consort is usually a dakini. As both consorts are Buddhas, these particular dakinis are fully awakened beings too. Not all dakinis are awakened beings, and Vajrayana Buddhism came to identify various other kinds, including dakinis in the original sense – who are very capricious and may or may not be helpful to tantric practitioners – and women who, because of their spiritual accomplishments, are regarded as dakinis in human form.

This suggests how dakinis may have become incorporated into the Buddhist tantra, but it does not explain why, as one of the three secret refuges, the dakini is the tantric embodiment of the Sangha refuge. We can trace this connection by exploring the meaning and symbolism of the dakini as an ideal awakened being. As far as the practitioner is concerned, generally speaking all tantric deities manifest on two levels – external and internal. Externally, there is the transcendental being, the awakened form, which we perceive – at least to begin with – as separate from ourselves. Internally, we progressively realize for ourselves the very qualities that the deity embodies, and so in this sense ultimately 'become' that deity. The further this process goes, the more the external and internal aspects coincide.

Externally, there are innumerable dakini forms – wrathful, semi-wrathful, and peaceful, some unbelievably ugly and some breathtakingly beautiful. Some have human – or more-or-less human – features, others have the heads of birds or animals. Dakinis are usually naked, with long, dishevelled hair, and wear ornaments made of human bone; some are draped with the skins of fierce animals. Their bodies may be green, yellow, blue, black, white, or, perhaps most characteristically, brilliant blood-red, and they hold ritual tantric implements. They are usually depicted dancing ecstatically in the sky (the Tibetan word for dakini can be translated 'sky goer' or 'sky dancer'), and surrounded by an aureole of flames.

For the tantric practitioner, every one of these elements has many layers of symbolic meaning. To suggest just a few, the dakini's nakedness suggests her total freedom from the constraints of the unawakened mind, while her bone ornaments symbolize the 'death' of the deluded self as an adornment. Her passionate appearance, dishevelled hair (and, in the case of one of the best-known dakinis, Vajrayogini, her blood-red body), and the aureole of flames, symbolize her great bliss and total unrestrained involvement in – and abandonment to – the spiritual life.

The symbolic meanings of the external form of the dakini feed into her inner significance for the tantric practitioner, who seeks to embody, ultimately, all the qualities of her fully awakened form – and experience an ever-increasing energy of pure, selfless inspiration that incorporates the heights and depths of being, integrating and transforming them in the blissful alchemical fire of insight. Inevitably, these qualities also transform the practitioner's relations with other people, including not only the vajra-guru but also their vajra-brothers and vajra-sisters – those who practise under the same guru or within the same lineage of tantric teachings.

The inner qualities of the dakini are, in other words, those that ideally characterize communication within the tantric sangha – indeed, not only within the tantric sangha, but within the Sangha generally. Such communication would embody the dakini's total wholeheartedness, unrestrained and selfless abandonment to Reality, freedom from conventional constraints, and an intimacy of the kind which, for most people, is experienced only with a lover (for the dakini is a consort too) – but without any sticky attachment or emotional complication, for this passion is channelled solely into the mutual quest for awakening.

Such qualities are ideals towards which spiritual friends within the Sangha can aspire, even though they will only be exemplified to the fullest degree between members of the Arya-Sangha. To the extent that we can embody and express dakini-like qualities in our spiritual and other friendships – irrespective of the sex of our friends – we experience the essence of sangha. Seen in this way (and there are innumerable ways of regarding dakinis), the dakini represents the person – or people – who most strongly inspire and motivate us to live the spiritual life, practise the spiritual path, and realize the spiritual goal. The deepest and most meaningful levels of human communication are themselves a dance of the dakini.

This brief outline of tantric Buddhism has covered only a fraction of its scope, and hasn't even mentioned many important elements and practices. However, just as the essence of Buddhism in general is the Three Jewels, so the essence of the Vajrayana is the three secret refuges – which are, of course, nothing but the tantra's particular perspective on, or re-statement of, the essential principles of the Three Jewels. The validity of the Vajrayana approach – as with all kinds of Buddhism – lies not in an outward conformity to the forms that Buddhism originally took on, but in its effectiveness as a way to awakening.

AFTERWORD

AT THE BEGINNING of the book, I posed the question 'What is it that Westerners today find attractive about Buddhism?' I hope that this book has provided some answers, and suggested how Buddhist teachings can be relevant to our lives here and now – even when they are expressed through the apparently bizarre images and conceptions of tantric Buddhism.

Over the two-and-a-half-thousand years of its existence, Buddhism has developed a wide range of schools, systems of practice, and kinds of sangha. Yet all of these expressions of the Dharma, however different from the earliest known forms of Buddhism they appear to be, stem from a single source – the awakened mind of the Buddha. This is not to say that every development in the expression of the Dharma, let alone every kind of Buddhism, could have been foreseen by the Buddha himself. The historical Buddha, Siddhartha Gautama, has a unique place in Buddhist and human history. He was – as far as Buddhists are concerned – the first human being to realize awakening *and* lead others to realize it. He 'opened the doors to the deathless' for all humanity. But having done this, he stood back. He did not place himself, as an individual personality, at the centre of his teaching.

Even so, after his death the Buddha's followers began to regard him in more and more exalted terms and even to treat him rather as if he were a god. In a sense, such developments were quite appropriate. After all, the Buddha was definitely not just an ordinary human being. By virtue of his awakening, it could be said, the Buddha became something more than human. Or – what perhaps amounts to the same thing – we could say that he became human in the fullest possible sense. Whatever the case, his followers from the earliest times right down to the present have wanted to express their feelings of reverence, gratitude, and even awe towards the person who opened up the possibility of awakening for all humanity. The Buddha himself did not, in any case, discourage his disciples from expressing their respect and veneration of him, but he always insisted that the Dharma was their main refuge. This comes across strongly in the Pali canon's account of the Buddha's final days.

Forty to fifty years had passed since his awakening, and the Buddha had now turned eighty. He was in the course of a lengthy walking tour, attended still by his cousin and faithful friend Ananda, to places where his disciples were staying. During this tour, it became clear to the Buddha that he would soon die – his body, like any other conditioned thing, was wearing out. During the rainy season, he became so ill that Ananda feared he would die any day, but, thinking of all the disciples he still wished to see, the Buddha willed himself to overcome the symptoms so that he could complete his tour and give his final teachings. On seeing this apparent recovery, a relieved Ananda told the Buddha that the only thing that had comforted him during the illness was the thought that the Buddha would not allow himself to die without making a pronouncement about the future of the Sangha.

The Buddha, however, told Ananda that he had no such intention. He had already passed on the Dharma, he said, without holding anything back. Now the Sangha was capable of managing its affairs without him. For his own part, said the Buddha, his body was like an old cart that was held together with bits of rope. Only by entering deep meditative states could he find freedom from the chronic physical pain. But his followers were quite able to be self-sufficient; all they had to do was go for refuge wholeheartedly to the Dharma and seek no refuge elsewhere. Clearly, the Buddha knew that his job was done – he had communicated the Dharma fully. As long as they developed knowledge, experience, and realization of the Dharma, his followers and their successors could flourish just as well without him as with him.

The Buddha and Ananda then continued their journey. A few weeks later, having seen many of his disciples for the last time, the Buddha reached a place called Kushinagara, and there he stopped. Stretched on his side between two flowering trees, he gave his final encouragement to the disciples who gathered round him at this solemn moment: 'Do not think that you no longer have a teacher,' he said, 'the Dharma and discipline I have taught are your teacher.' He then asked whether any of the assembled bhikshus had any doubts concerning the Buddha, the Dharma, the Sangha, or the path to awakening. No one said a word. Seeing that he truly had nothing left to do, the Buddha spoke his very last words: 'All conditioned things are impermanent. With mindfulness, strive.'

After that, the Buddha died and passed beyond ordinary human perception. But the Dharma continued – and still continues – to live. It lives most fully, of course, in those who have realized it – the Arya-Sangha of awakened human beings and those irreversibly on the path to awakening. The state of awakening is the same for all who realize it, and transcends time and space. Similarly, all authentic expressions of the Dharma, all the new forms of Buddhism initiated to suit the needs of particular cultures and times, stem from the same source. It is this confluence between the universal and the specific, the awakened mind and the particular conditions of time and place, that allows Buddhism to remain true to the Buddha's vision while embracing the diversity of human life.

Like all things, Buddhism is subject to impermanence, and its many forms have continued to develop and change, grow, and decay. The state of Buddhism in the world a century ago could hardly be more different from its condition today. From one point of view, the last hundred years could be seen as quite disastrous. In particular, militant communism has attacked Buddhism and severely weakened it in vast areas where it traditionally flourished, including China, Tibet, Mongolia, Vietnam, Cambodia, and North Korea. Elsewhere, it has often been weakened by materialism, or simply by internal atrophy.

And yet, paradoxically, Buddhism is now truly a worldwide religion for the first time. Even in those parts of the world where it is a traditional part of the culture, the story of the last hundred years is by no means entirely one of decay. There have been some quite startling areas of growth, and new sanghas and new forms of Buddhism have emerged. Even the inhospitable political climate in China has not succeeded in wiping out grass-roots Buddhism. Meanwhile, traditional forms – especially Theravada, Zen, and Tibetan Buddhism

– have spread to every continent, and practically every country, worldwide. Ironically, in the case of Tibet, it was the Chninese invasion and occupation itself which hastened the spread of Tibetan Buddhism in the rest of the world by forcing the Dalai Lama and many other Buddhist teachers into exile.

Other forms of Buddhism have been no less active. Some sources claim that the practice of Zen is now at least as strong in the United States as it is in Japan. There are at any rate practitioners of Zen (or Ch'an), as well as Theravada Buddhism, in most Western towns and cities, as well as in many rural centres. Nichiren, Shin, and other forms of Mahayana Buddhism have also spread around the world. And at least one sangha has arisen in the West which is not a derivation of any of the traditional schools but looks to Buddhist tradition overall for its sources: the Western Buddhist Order, founded in the late 1960s by the English Buddhist, Sangharakshita.

So although there may now be fewer Buddhists overall than there were in 1900, Buddhism itself is accessible – and visible – to a far larger proportion of the world's population than ever before. Anybody interested, practically anywhere in the world, can easily obtain information and literature about Buddhism. If someone in the West wants to meet practising Buddhists, receive teachings on Buddhism or meditation, or encounter an active sangha, they no longer have to set off for the other side of the world – Buddhists could well be living locally. Buddhism has an immense amount to offer humanity. And today, perhaps more than ever before, it has a real opportunity to change the world – if, that is, we are willing to change ourselves.

GLOSSARY

Ideally, this book would have been written entirely in English. However, there are good reasons for including in a book such as this selected terms from the Buddhist canonical languages of Pāli and Sanskrit. A number of such terms are already to be found in English dictionaries, while some of the more technical terms are difficult to render into a satisfactory single-word English equivalent. Also, many of the Sanskrit and Pāli words in this book are proper nouns. In order to make matters as simple as possible, I have with a few exceptions used Sanskrit, even when discussing the Theravāda school and its collection of scriptures – the Pāli canon. The exceptions are some Pāli words which are becoming anglicized in their own right, such as *mettā* rather than the Sanskrit *maitrī*, and *samatha* and *vipassanā* rather than the Sanskrit *śamatha* and *vipaśyanā*.

For those who want to know how Sanskrit and Pāli words are pronounced, or wish to look them up elsewhere, those from the text are included in this glossary with the diacritical marks that indicate the correct spelling and pronunciation. Vowels with a macron (ā, ī, ū) are long; this is worth noting, as long vowels in Sanskrit and Pāli are not always where English speakers would expect them to be. The letters ś and ṣ have both been rendered 'sh', and 'c' has been rendered 'ch', which is roughly how they sound. A full pronunciation guide is included in *A Concise History of Buddhism* by Andrew Skilton (see Further Reading). The explanations below are intended mostly as a reminder, rather than as full definitions.

Readers are likely to encounter Pāli equivalents in other books on Buddhism, so some have been included following the Sanskrit, but unless otherwise indicated all the terms are Sanskrit. When a different spelling is employed in the text this is shown in brackets. The Tibetan words in the glossary are spelt to suggest their pronunciation, with the correct form following it in brackets.

Abhidharma (Sanskrit), *abhidhamma* (Pāli)
'Pure dharma', a systematization of the Buddha's teachings on wisdom in essential form. It may or may not be canonical, depending on school.

Abhirati
'Supreme joy', the pure Buddha realm of Akṣobhya.

Akṣobhya (Akshobhya)
'Imperturbable', an archetypal Buddha of the Mahayana and Vajrayana.

Amitābha
'Infinite light', an archetypal Buddha of the Mahayana and Vajrayana.

Amitāyus
'Infinite life', a manifestation of Amitābha.

anātman
'not-self' or, less literally, 'insubstantiality', 'selflessness'.

arhant (Sanskrit), *arahant* (Pāli)
'Worthy one', an epithet for an awakened person.

ārya
'Noble one', an epithet for someone who has achieved irreversibility from awakening (stream entry), or any higher level of realization.

āryasangha (Arya-Sangha)
The 'community' of *āryas*, the essence of the Sangha Jewel and Sangha refuge.

Asaṅga
The founder of the school known as Cittamātra or Yogācāra.

ātman
A very subtle metaphysical self-entity taught by some of the Buddha's contemporaries; now found in certain aspects of Hinduism.

Avalokiteśvara (Avalokiteshvara)
'The lord who looks (with compassion)', an archetypal Bodhisattva of the Mahāyāna and Vajrayāna, embodying awakened compassion.

Bāhiya
One of the Buddha's personal disciples.

bhāvanā
Meditation in the sense of the development or cultivation of particular qualities.

bhikṣu (bhikshu) *(masc.)*, *bhikṣunī* (bhikshuni) *(fem.)* (Sanskrit); *bhikkhu* *(masc.)*, *bhikkhunī (fem.)* (Pāli)
A mendicant, one who lives on alms-food, Buddhist monastic. Often referred to as a Buddhist monk or nun.

bodhi
Awakening, the awakened state.

Bodhisattva
'Awakening being', one who is set upon awakening. 1: An epithet of the Buddha in his previous lives and up to the moment of his awakening. 2: A follower of the Mahayana who aspires to the ideal of realizing awakening for the sake of all beings. 3: An archetypal figure exemplifying this ideal and usually embodying a particular quality of awakening, such as compassion or wisdom.

Buddha
An awakened being. 'The Buddha' usually connotes the historical founder of Buddhism, Siddhartha Gautama.

Ch'an (Chinese)
The 'dhyāna' school of Chinese Mahayana Buddhism, which later became the Zen school in Japan.

Cittamātra (Chittamatra)
'Mind only', a name of the Mahāyāna school also known as Yogācāra.

ḍāka
The male equivalent of a ḍākinī.

ḍākinī
Originally a cannibalistic ogress, in tantric Buddhism she became an archetypal figure, the embodiment of awakening, the tantric equivalent of the Sangha refuge. There are also mundane ḍākinīs – often more like the original cannibalistic ogresses, and human ḍākinīs, women who are regarded as ḍākinīs in human form.

deva
A being who exists on a higher or more subtle level, subject like humans to death and rebirth. Often translated as 'god'.

devatā
'Deity', the ideal awakened being who appears at the heart of tantric practices.

Dharma (Sanskrit), *Dhamma* (Pāli)
In the sense of Dharma Jewel and Dharma Refuge, Dharma is the truth, 'the way things really are'. Dharma also connotes the path to awakening. In *abhidharma* systems, 'dharma' is also used to mean 'ultimate constituent'.

dhyāna
'Absorption'; also a general word for meditation.

Gautama
The family name of the historical Buddha.

guru
In Vajrayāna, the master (male or female) who confers tantric initiation, enabling a disciple to engage in the practices of a particular tantric meditation system.

hatha yoga
'Yoga' in the sense it is usually understood in the West, comprising *āsanas* (postures) and *praṇayāma* (breathing exercises). This derives from Hindu sources, but there are Buddhist equivalents in the tantric systems.

Hīnayāna
'Lesser' or 'inferior' way, a term used by early Mahayanists to describe pre-Mahāyāna schools of Buddhism.

Jātakas
A collection of stories describing the previous lives of the Buddha.

Jina
'Conqueror', an epithet of the Buddha.

kalyāṇa
'Beautiful', 'noble', 'virtuous', 'good'.

kalyāṇa mitratā
Friendship with the beautiful, etc., or friendship which is beautiful, etc.

Kapilavastu
The birthplace of the Buddha, in present-day southern Nepal.

Karma
'Action', volitional action which, by virtue of its skilfulness or unskilfulness, forms or determines what sort of person we become.

kōan (Japanese)
A paradox that cannot be resolved on the level of the rational mind.

Kondañña
The Buddha's first awakened disciple.

kula
In tantric Buddhism, a community of initiates of the same guru, or practitioners of the same tantra.

Kuśinagara (Kushinagara)
Site of the Buddha's death or *parinirvāṇa*.

Lama (Tibetan: *bla ma*)
The Tibetan equivalent of 'guru'.

Madhyamaka
'Middling' or 'middle way'. A Mahāyāna school tracing its origins to the writings of Nagārjuna.

Mahāprajāpatī
Aunt and foster-mother of Siddhartha Gautama.

mahāsangha (Maha-Sangha)
'Great sangha', the all-inclusive Mahāyāna sangha which consists of both monastics and laypeople.

mahāsiddha
'Great adept', a person who has gained awakening through Vajrayāna practices.

Mahāyāna
'Great way', originally used in contradistinction to the Hīnayāna, but now connoting any school of Buddhism that regards Mahayana sūtras as the authentic word of the Buddha.

Maitreya (Sanskrit), *Metteya* (Pāli)
'The loving one'. An archetypal Bodhisattva who is predicted to become the next Buddha in a distant future age when the Dharma has completely disappeared from the world.

Maitreya (sometimes called *Maitreyanātha*)
Possibly the teacher of Asaṅga.

maṇḍala
'Circle', in the sense of 'circle of deities' visualized surrounding the central deity (*devatā*) in tantric meditation practices. Also, a two- or three-dimensional representation of this, used in tantric initiations.

Mañjuśrī (Manjushri)
'Gentle radiance', an archetypal Bodhisattva of the Mahāyāna and Vajrayāna, embodying perfect wisdom.

mantra
A 'symbol in sound', embodying qualities of a particular archetypal Buddha, Bodhisattva, or tantric deity.

Meghiya (Pāli)
One of the Buddha's personal disciples.

mettā (Pāli), *maitrī* (Sanskrit)
Friendliness, disinterested love, loving-kindness.

mudrā
A ritual gesture used in tantric Buddhism.

Nagārjuna
The founder of the Madhyamaka school of Mahāyāna Buddhism.

nidāna
In the formula of conditioned arising, the link between one conditioning factor and another that arises in dependence upon it.

nirvāṇa
The 'going out' of the fires of craving, aversion, and delusion, tantamount to awakening.

oṁ maṇi padme hūṁ
The mantra of Avalokiteśvara.

Pāli
The canonical language of the Theravāda school.

parinirvāṇa
The Buddha's entry into 'final nirvāṇa' at the time of his death.

Piṅgiya (Pāli)
One of the Buddha's personal disciples.

prajñā (Sanskrit), *paññā* (Pāli)
Wisdom, understanding.

prātimokṣa (pratimoksha) (Sanskrit), *pāṭimokkha* (Pāli)
The core set of rules of each monastic sangha.

pūjā
'Worship'. A general term for a Buddhist devotional ceremony.

Rāhula
The son of Siddhartha Gautama.

sādhana
In Vajrayāna, a set form in which the meditative and ritual practices involved in a particular tantra are to be carried out.

Śākya (Shakya)
The clan name of the historical Buddha.

Śākyamuni (Shakyamuni)
'Sage of the Śākyas', an epithet for the Buddha, particularly in Mahāyāna Buddhism.

samādhi
Meditative concentration, any meditative state, a state of insight, awakening.

samatha (Pāli)
Tranquillity, or calm.

samatha-bhāvanā (Pāli)
The cultivation of tranquillity, tranquillity meditation.

Saṁsāra
The unawakened state, cyclic existence, the round of constant rebirth resulting from delusion.

Sangha
The Buddhist spiritual community. 1: As the Sangha Jewel and Sangha refuge, it indicates primarily the *āryasangha*. 2: Any established Buddhist community. 3: The monastic community (Theravāda).

Sarvāstivāda
An early (pre-Mahāyāna) school.

Siddhārtha
The personal name of the Buddha.

śraddhā (shraddha)
'Faith' in the sense of confidence and trust in the Buddha's teaching.

stūpa
A characteristic Buddhist monument, sometimes holding relics of the Buddha or other awakened person or the remains of any deceased Buddhist.

Sukhāvatī
'The blissful', the pure Buddha realm of Amitābha.

śūnyatā (shunyata)
Emptiness, voidness, absence of 'true existence' in any phenomena.

sūtra (Sanskrit), *sutta* (Pāli)
In the canon of any particular school, a text (or oral transmission) regarded as the authentic teaching of the Buddha, or authenticated by the Buddha.

Sutta Nipāta
One of the oldest portions of the Pāli Canon.

tantra
A canonical tantric or Vajrayāna text containing the teachings of a particular tantric system.

Tārā
'She who ferries across'. An archetypal Bodhisattva of the late Mahāyāna and Vajrayāna, embodying awakened compassion.

Tathāgata
The 'thus-come' or 'thus-gone', an epithet of the Buddha.

Tathāgatagarbha
The 'Buddha within' school of Mahāyāna Buddhism.

Theravāda (Pāli)
'Teaching of the elders', a major school of Buddhism, the only surviving non-Mahāyāna school.

Theravādin
A follower of the Theravāda.

tulku (Tibetan: *sprul sku*)
An Tibetan incarnate lama.

upāsaka (masc.), upasikā (fem.)
'One who sits near (the teacher)'. Non-renunciate followers, householder followers, lay Buddhists.

vajra
Adamantine-thunderbolt. In the Vajrayāna, a symbol of reality or *śūnyatā*.

Vajradhāra
'Holder of the vajra'. An archetypal Buddha of the Vajrayāna, regarded in some systems as the form taken by Śākyamuni Buddha in order to teach the tantras.

Vajrapāṇi
'Vajra-in-hand', or 'he who holds the vajra'. An archetypal Bodhisattva of the Mahāyāna and, particularly, the Vajrayāna, embodying awakened energy.

Vajrasattva
'Vajra-being', an archetypal Buddha of the Vajrayāna, embodying the essentially pure and empty 'vajra-nature' of all beings.

Vajrayāna
'Way of the vajra', used here in reference to the Buddhist tantra in general. According to some sources, it applies only to the inner tantras.

Vajrayoginī
An archetypal awakened ḍākinī of the Vajrayāna.

Vinaya Piṭaka (Pāli)
The collection of discourses on monastic discipline.

vipassanā (Pāli), *vipaśyanā* (Sanskrit)
Insight.

vipassanā-bhāvanā (Pāli)
The cultivation of insight, insight meditation.

yidam (Tibetan: *yi dam*)
'Oath-bound'. The Tibetan equivalent of *devatā*.

Yogācāra (Yogachara)
'The way of yoga'. An alternative name for the Cittamātra school of
Mahāyāna Buddhism.

yogi or *yogin (masc.), yoginī (fem.)*
'Practitioner of yoga'. In Vajrayāna, an epithet for a tantric practitioner.

NOTES

1 Bhikkhu Ñāṇamoli, *The Life of the Buddha*, Buddhist Publication Society, Kandy 1992, p.52 (slightly amended).

2 *The Minor Anthologies of the Pali Canon, Part II, Udāna: Verses of Uplift*, trans. F.L. Woodward, OUP, London 1948.

3 ibid. (slightly amended.)

4 In Pali, metta.

5 *Dhammapada* 5.

6 Quoted in Paul Reps, *Zen Flesh, Zen Bones*, Penguin, Harmondsworth, 1971.

7 ibid.

8 Sutras are canonical texts, usually in the form of discourses given by the Buddha – the same as *sutta* in Pali.

9 *Dhammapada* 188–92.

10 'Bhikkhu' is the Pali equivalent of 'bhikshu'.

11 L. Hurvitz, *Scripture of the Lotus Blossom of the Fine Dharma (The Lotus Sutra)*, translated from the Chinese of Kumarajiva, Columbia University Press, New York 1976, p.29.

12 K.R. Norman (trans.), *The Rhinoceros Horn and Other Early Buddhist Poems*, Pali Text Society, London 1985, p.184.

13 Sthiramati's *Madhyantavibhagatika*, quoted in Paul Williams, *Mahāyāna Buddhism*, Routledge, London and New York 1989, p.89. (Quotation slightly modified.)

14 Quoted in: Bhikkhu Ñāṇananda, *Concept and Reality in Early Buddhist Thought*, Kandy 1971, p.65.

FURTHER READING

BUDDHIST TEXTS

The Dhammapada. Several translations of this important Pali text are available. The version by J. Mascaro (Penguin, Harmonsworth 1973) is easily available, but not entirely reliable. The translation by Buddharakkhita Thera is fairly dependable.

The Diamond Sutra and The Sutra of Hui Neng, Shambhala, Boston 1990. An important Mahayana sutra together with a classic text of Ch'an Buddhism.

E. Conze, *Buddhist Texts Through the Ages*, Oneworld, Oxford 1995. A useful selection of texts from most major Buddhist schools.

L. Hurvitz, *Scripture of the Lotus Blossom of the Fine Dharma*, translated from the Chinese of Kumarajiva, Columbia University Press, New York 1976. A translation of the famous *Lotus Sutra*, one of the most influential of all Mahayana sutras.

Lobsang P. Lhalungpa, *The Life of Milarepa*, Book Faith India, Kathmandu 1997. A very readable translation of a classic spiritual biography and an excellent introduction to the spirit of the Vajrayana in Tibet.

Bhikkhu Ñāṇamoli, *The Life of the Buddha*, Buddhist Publication Society, Kandy 1992. An excellent compilation from the Pali canon.

Śāntideva, *Bodhicāryavatāra*, Kate Crosby and Andrew Skilton (trans.), OUP, Oxford 1996. A beautiful, and influential, exposition of the Mahayana path, by the eighth-century poet.

Robert A.F. Thurman (trans.), *The Holy Teaching of Vimalakīrti: A Mahāyāna Scripture*, Pennsylvania State University Press, Pennsylvania and London 1976. An excellent translation of a major Mahayana sutra.

Maurice Walshe (trans.), *Long Discourses of the Buddha*, Wisdom, Boston 1995. A readable translation of one of the most important sections of the Pali canon.

BOOKS ABOUT BUDDHISM

Stephen Batchelor, *The Awakening of the West*, HarperCollins, London 1994. How Buddhism came to Europe – very readable.

Rick Fields, *How the Swans Came to the Lake*, Shambhala, Boston 1981. How Buddhism came to America – also very readable.

Kamalashila, *Meditation*, Windhorse, Birmingham 1996. A very practical survey of the whole field of Buddhist meditation, except Vajrayana.

Philip Kapleau, *The Three Pillars of Zen*, Weatherhill, Tokyo, 1965. A popular introduction by a highly-regarded Western Zen teacher.

John Powers, *Introduction to Tibetan Buddhism*, Snow Lion, Ithaca 1995. A thorough and straightforward introduction.

Walpola Rahula, *What the Buddha Taught*, Oneworld, Oxford 1997. A straightforward introduction to Buddhist teaching according to the Theravada school.

Sangharakshita, *A Survey of Buddhism*, Windhorse, Glasgow 1993. The seventh edition of a classic survey and detailed exposition of many fundamental Buddhist doctrines.

Andrew Skilton, *A Concise History of Buddhism*, Windhorse, Birmingham 1997. An excellent overview of Buddhist history and schools, with a very extensive and useful bibliography.

Paul Williams, *Mahāyāna Buddhism*, Routledge, London and New York 1989. A scholarly book, by far the best general survey of the Mahayana schools and teachings.

INDEX

The Windhorse symbolizes the energy of the enlightened mind carrying the Three Jewels – the Buddha, the Dharma, and the Sangha – to all sentient beings.

Buddhism is one of the fastest-growing spiritual traditions in the Western world. Throughout its 2,500-year history, it has always succeeded in adapting its mode of expression to suit whatever culture it has encountered.

Windhorse Publications aims to continue this tradition as Buddhism comes to the West. Today's Westerners are heirs to the entire Buddhist tradition, free to draw instruction and inspiration from all the many schools and branches. Windhorse publishes works by authors who not only understand the Buddhist tradition but are also familiar with Western culture and the Western mind.

For orders and catalogues contact

WINDHORSE PUBLICATIONS
11 PARK ROAD
BIRMINGHAM
B13 8AB
UK

WINDHORSE BOOKS
P O BOX 574
NEWTOWN
NSW 2042
AUSTRALIA

Windhorse Publications is an arm of the Friends of the Western Buddhist Order, which has more than sixty centres on five continents. Through these centres, members of the Western Buddhist Order offer regular programmes of events for the general public and for more experienced students. These include meditation classes, public talks, study on Buddhist themes and texts, and 'bodywork' classes such as t'ai chi, yoga, and massage. The FWBO also runs several retreat centres and the Karuna Trust, a fund-raising charity that supports social welfare projects in the slums and villages of India.

Many FWBO centres have residential spiritual communities and ethical businesses associated with them. Arts activities are encouraged too, as is the development of strong bonds of friendship between people who share the same ideals. In this way the FWBO is developing a unique approach to Buddhism, not simply as a set of techniques, less still as an exotic cultural interest, but as a creatively directed way of life for people living in the modern world.

If you would like more information about the FWBO please write to

LONDON BUDDHIST CENTRE
51 ROMAN ROAD
LONDON
E2 0HU
UK

ARYALOKA
HEARTWOOD CIRCLE
NEWMARKET
NH 03857
USA

ALSO FROM WINDHORSE

SANGHARAKSHITA

A GUIDE TO THE BUDDHIST PATH

Which Buddhist teachings really matter? How does one begin to practise them in a systematic way? Without a guide one can easily get dispirited or lost.

In this highly readable anthology a leading Western Buddhist sorts out fact from myth, essence from cultural accident, to reveal the fundamental ideals and teachings of Buddhism. The result is a reliable map of the Buddhist path that anyone can follow.

Sangharakshita is an ideal companion on the path. As founder of a major Western Buddhist movement he has helped thousands of people to make an effective contact with the richness and beauty of the Buddha's teachings.

256 pages, with illustrations
ISBN 1 899579 04 4
£12.50/$24.95

PARAMANANDA

CHANGE YOUR MIND: A PRACTICAL GUIDE TO BUDDHIST MEDITATION

Buddhism is based on the truth that, with effort, we can change the way we are. But how? Among the many methods Buddhism has to offer, meditation is the most direct. It is the art of getting to know one's own mind and learning to encourage what is best in us.

This is an accessible and thorough guide to meditation, based on traditional material but written in a light and modern style. Colourfully illustrated with anecdotes and tips from the author's experience as a meditator and teacher, it also offers refreshing inspiration to seasoned meditators.

208 pages, with photographs
ISBN 0 904766 81 0
£8.50/$16.95

RICHARD P. HAYES

LAND OF NO BUDDHA:

REFLECTIONS OF A SCEPTICAL BUDDHIST

Witty, honest, and thought-provoking, Richard Hayes casts a critical eye over modern society and the teachings of Buddhism as they flow into the West. Written with the perspective that comes from more than twenty years of study and practice, *Land of No Buddha* examines the pitfalls awaiting those who search for the truth. A sceptical Buddhist, Hayes nevertheless proposes the radical path of the Buddha – becoming free from self-indulgent passions and delusions – to those seeking genuine wisdom, not just slogans to stick on the bumpers of their cars.

288 pages
ISBN 1 899579 12 5
£9.99/$19.95

P.D. RYAN

BUDDHISM AND THE NATURAL WORLD:

TOWARDS A MEANINGFUL MYTH

P.D. Ryan takes a fresh look at our relationship with the living world and offers a radical analysis of our consumerist attitudes. Applying the Buddha's fundamental message of non-violence to these crucial issues, he draws out a middle way between destructiveness and sentimentality: a way which recognizes the truth of the interdependence of all life and places universal compassion at the very centre of our relationship with the world.

In *Buddhism and the Natural World* Ryan emphasizes the importance of living in accord with this truth – and reminds us of the Buddha's insistence that to do so calls for nothing less than a revolution in consciousness.

144 pages
ISBN 1 899579 00 1
£6.99/$13.95

SANGHARAKSHITA

THE ESSENCE OF ZEN

A special transmission outside the scriptures;
No dependence on words and letters;
Direct pointing to the mind;
Seeing into one's own nature and realizing Buddhahood.

Each of these lines represents a fundamental principle of the Zen or Ch'an School of Buddhism. But what do they mean? And can they be practised in the West?

Sangharakshita, a leading figure in the modern Buddhist world, draws on his knowledge and long practice of Buddhism to reflect on each line in turn, communicating its essence and indicating how we can apply its meaning to Western life.

64 pages
ISBN 0 904766 91 8
£4.99/$8.95

SANGHARAKSHITA

THE TEN PILLARS OF BUDDHISM

The Ten Pillars of Buddhism are ten ethical principles which together provide a comprehensive guide to the moral dimension of human life.

To explore them is to turn the lens of moral vision on to one aspect of life after another. To apply them is to accept the challenge of human potential for higher development – and to work with that challenge in the arena of everyday life.

Readers from the Buddhist world will find some of Sangharakshita's ideas especially thought-provoking – and even controversial. But all readers, whether Buddhists or not, will find this essay an invaluable source of stimulation and insight in their quest for ethical standards by which to live.

112 pages
ISBN 1 899579 21 4
£5.99/$11.95

SANGHARAKSHITA

THE THREE JEWELS: THE CENTRAL IDEALS OF BUDDHISM

The Three Jewels are living symbols, supreme objects of commitment and devotion in the life of every Buddhist.

This authoritative book, by an outstanding Western Buddhist teacher, explains the pivotal importance of the Three Jewels. To understand the Three Jewels is to understand the central ideals and principles of Buddhism. To have some insight into them is to touch its very heart.

264 pages
ISBN 1 899579 06 0
£11.99/$23.95

SANGHARAKSHITA

TIBETAN BUDDHISM: AN INTRODUCTION

A glorious past, a traumatic present, an uncertain future. What are we to make of Tibetan Buddhism?

Sangharakshita has spent many years in contact with Tibetan lamas of all schools, within the context of a wide experience of the Buddhist tradition as a whole. He is admirably qualified as a guide through the labyrinth that is Tibetan Buddhism. In this book he gives a down-to-earth account of the origin and history of Buddhism in Tibet, and explains the essentials of this practical tradition which has much to teach us.

As the essence of Tibetan Buddhism is revealed, it is shown to be a beautiful and noble tradition which – and this is the important thing – can help us contact a sense of beauty and nobility in our lives.

144 pages, illustrated
ISBN 0 904766 86 1
£7.99/$15.95

KALYANAVACA (editor)

THE MOON AND FLOWERS: A WOMAN'S PATH TO ENLIGHTENMENT

This book brings together essays by nineteen women who have been ordained within the Buddhist tradition. They come from different countries and have very different lifestyles. Their firm commitment to Buddhism is perhaps the only thing they all have in common.

Here they demonstrate how they are trying to bring the various aspects and concerns of their daily lives into harmony with their Buddhist ideals and practice. They talk about feminism, motherhood, work, sexuality, friendship, and many other issues. The wide variety of personal experience woven together with key principles and practices makes for a vivid and richly textured portrait of what it means to follow the Buddhist path as a woman in the modern world.

304 pages, with photographs
ISBN 0 904766 89 6
£11.99/$23.95

VESSANTARA

MEETING THE BUDDHAS:

A GUIDE TO BUDDHAS, BODHISATTVAS, AND TANTRIC DEITIES

Sitting poised and serene upon fragrant lotus blooms, they offer smiles of infinite tenderness, immeasurable wisdom. Bellowing formidable roars of angry triumph from the heart of blazing infernos, they dance on the naked corpses of their enemies.

Who are these beings – the Buddhas, Bodhisattvas, and Protectors, the 'angry demons' and 'benign deities' – of the Buddhist Tantric tradition? Are they products of an alien, even disturbed, imagination? Or are they, perhaps, real? What have they got to do with Buddhism? And what have they got to do with us?

In this vivid informed account, an experienced Western Buddhist guides us into the heart of this magical realm and introduces us to the miraculous beings who dwell there.

368 pages, with text illustrations and colour plates
ISBN 0 904766 53 5
£14.99/$29.95